The Story of Cambridge

STEPHANIE BOYD

CAMBRIDGE
UNIVERSITY PRESS

CAMBRIDGE
UNIVERSITY PRESS

For Alexander and Helena

University Printing House, Cambridge CB2 8BS, United Kingdom

One Liberty Plaza, 20th Floor, New York, NY 10006, USA

477 Williamstown Road, Port Melbourne, VIC 3207, Australia

314-321, 3rd Floor, Plot 3, Splendor Forum, Jasola District Centre, New Delhi - 110025, India

103 Penang Road, #05-06/07, Visioncrest Commercial, Singapore 238467

Cambridge University Press is part of the University of Cambridge.

It furthers the University's mission by disseminating knowledge in the pursuit of
education, learning and research at the highest international levels of excellence.

www.cambridge.org
Information on this title: www.cambridge.org/9780521628976

First published 2005
Republished with corrections 2006
11th printing 2019

A catalogue record for this publication is available from the British Library

ISBN 978-0-521-62897-6 Paperback

Acknowledgements

p.1 Left, centre & right, ©Hart McLeod, p.4 Bottom, ©Hart McLeod, p.5 Bottom, ©Hart McLeod, p.6 Centre left, ©University Museum of Archaeology and Anthropology, top right, ©Sedgwick Museum, Cambridge, centre bottom, ©Cambridge University Department of Earth Sciences; p.7 Bottom left, ©University Museum of Archaeology and Anthropology, bottom right ©University Museum of Archaeology and Anthropology; p.8 Bottom right, ©University Museum of Archaeology and Anthropology; p.9 Centre, ©Hart McLeod; p.10 top left, ©Alan Wyatt, centre bottom, ©Cambridge County Council Field Unit; p.11 Top left, ©Cambridge County Council Field Unit, bottom right, ©Hart McLeod; p.13 Gwill Owen at the Cambridge Archaeological unit; p.14 top left, ©Cambridge County Council Field Unit, centre right, ©Hart McLeod; p.15 Bottom left, ©Caroline Mallim, Archaeological Field Unit (CCC); p.16 Top right, ©The Trustees of the British Museum, right, ©Hart McLeod; p.17 Top right, ©Hart McLeod; p.18 Top, ©Hart McLeod; p.19 Top right, ©Mary Evans Picture Library, bottom left insert & bottom right, ©Hart McLeod; p.20 Top right, ©Cambridgeshire Collection, centre & bottom, ©Hart McLeod; p.21 Bottom left, ©Cambridgeshire Collection top & right ©Hart McLeod; p.22 Bottom right, ©Cambridgeshire Collection, top ©Hart McLeod; p.23 Bottom, ©Reproduced by kind permission of the Cambridge Evening News; p.24 Top right, ©The Monumental Brasses of Cambridge, bottom centre, ©Corpus Christi College, Cambridge, top left, ©Hart McLeod; p.25 Centre left, ©Queen's College, Cambridge, top right & bottom, ©Hart McLeod; p.26 Top, ©permission of the Syndics of Cambridge University Library. From Leedham-Green, E.S. A Concise History of the University of Cambridge. Cambridge University Press; p.27 Bottom right & Centre right, ©National Portrait Gallery, London, centre left & top, ©Hart McLeod; p.28 Top, ©King's College, Cambridge; p.29 full page, ©Reproduced with the permission of the Provost and Scholars of King's College, Cambridge; p.30 Bottom centre, ©Bridgeman Art Library, bottom left, ©AKG Images, bottom right, ©Queen's College, Cambridge, top right, ©Hart McLeod; p.31 Top left & bottom right, ©The Master and Fellows of Queens' College, Cambridge; p.32 Bottom right, ©The Master and Fellows of Queens' College Cambridge, top left ©Hart McLeod; p.33 Full page, ©Cambridgeshire Collection; p.34 Bottom left, ©The Masters of St John's College, bottom centre, ©Cambridge University Library, top right, ©Mary Evans Picture Library, Middle right, ©Fitzwilliam Museum, Cambridge, top left, ©Bridgeman Art Library, centre, ©Hart McLeod; p.35 Top left, top right & centre right, ©Reproduced with the permission of the Provost and Scholars of King's College, Cambridge, bottom right, ©Hart McLeod; p.36 Top left, ©Francis G. Mayer/Corbis; p.37 Top left, ©Mary Evans Picture Library, top centre, ©Bridgeman Art Library, bottom, ©Hart McLeod; p.38 Top, bottom & centre, ©Hart McLeod; p.39 Top centre, centre & bottom, ©Hart McLeod; p.40 Bottom left, ©National gallery collection, By kind permission of the Trustees of the National Gallery, London/Corbis, top left, ©Mary Evans Picture Library; p.41 Bottom left, ©The Bridgeman Art Library, top right, ©Country Life Picture Library, Top left, © The Bridgeman Art Library, top right, ©Hart McLeod; p.42 Bottom left & top right, ©permission of the Syndics of Cambridge University

Library. From Leedham-Green, E.S. A Concise History of the University of Cambridge. Cambridge University Press; p.43 Bottom right, ©Topham Picturepoint/Topfoto.co.uk, top left, ©permission of the Master and Fellows of Emmanuel College, Cambridge, bottom left, ©Hart McLeod; p.44 Bottom right, ©Science Museum, London/HIP/Topfoto.co.uk, Bottom left, ©Chris Andrews; Chris Andrews Publications/Corbis; p.45 Top right, centre & bottom, ©Hart McLeod; p.46 Bottom right, ©Bettmann/Corbis, centre left, ©AKG Images, bottom left, ©The Cromwell Museum, Huntingdon, centre right, ©Hart McLeod; p.47 Top right, ©Cambridgeshire Collection, bottom right, ©Sidney Sussex College, Centre, ©Trinity College Cambridge; p.48 Insert, ©Mary Evans Picture Library, bottom & top, ©Hart McLeod; p.49 Top right, ©Bridgeman Art Library, centre, bottom right, bottom left, left insert, ©Hart McLeod; p.50 Top left, ©permission of the Syndics of Cambridge University Library. From Leedham-Green, E.S. A Concise History of the University of Cambridge. Cambridge University Press, centre, ©Hart McLeod; p.51 Top left, top right & bottom left, ©Hart McLeod p.52 Bottom, ©Cambridgeshire Collection, top right, ©Hart McLeod, p.53 Centre right, bottom left, bottom right ©Cambridgeshire Collection, centre left, ©The Royal Armouries Museum, Leeds, top left, ©Cambridgeshire Collection; p.54 Top left, bottom right, ©Cambridgeshire Collection; p.55 Top & bottom. ©Bridgeman Picture Library; p.56 Centre left, Bottom, ©Cambridgeshire Collection; p.58 Centre, ©Bettmann/Corbis, top right, ©Bridgeman Picture Library; p.59 Top ©Bettmann/Corbis, Bottom left, ©Cambridgeshire Collection, top centre right, ©University Museum of Zoology, Cambridge, bottom right & centre ©Hart McLeod; p.60 Top, ©The Mistress and Fellows, Girton College, Cambridge, bottom left, ©Hart McLeod; p.61 Top, ©Cambridgeshire Collection, bottom, ©The Principle and Fellows, Newnham College, Cambridge; p.62 Top, ©Cambridgeshire Collection, centre right, ©The Cambridge Collection; p.63 Top left, top right, bottom left, ©Cambridgeshire Collection, bottom right, bottom right, ©Hart McLeod; p.64 Top right, ©The Mistress and Fellows, Girton College, Cambridge, bottom left & bottom right, ©The Cavendish Laboratory, University of Cambridge, centre right, © Richard Summers, Wellcome Trust Sanger Institute; p.65 Bottom left, ©Popperfoto/ alamy.com, top right, ©Hulton-Deutsch Collection/Corbis, centre left & centre right, ©The Cavendish Laboratory, University of Cambridge, bottom right, ©Hart McLeod; p.66 Top left, ©Hulton-Deutsch Collection/Corbis, centre ©Bettmann/Corbis, bottom, ©Conde Nast Archive/Corbis; p.67 Centre left, ©Hulton-Deutsch Collection/Corbis, Top right, bottom, ©Cambridgeshire Collection, centre right, ©Hart McLeod; p.68 Bottom, ©Bettmann/Corbis, top right, ©Hart McLeod; p.69 Top, ©Gwen Raverat/Faber and Faber, bottom right, ©Reproduced by kind permission of the Cambridge Evening News, bottom left, ©Hart McLeod; p.70 Top, bottom, ©Cambridgeshire Collection; p.71 Bottom left, ©Cambridgeshire Collection, centre right, ©The Cambridge Collection, bottom right, ©Hart McLeod; p.72 Bottom, ©Swim Ink/Corbis, top left, ©Cambridgeshire Collection; p.73 Bottom, ©Bettman/Corbis, top & centre left, ©Cambridgeshire Collection; p.74 Right, ©Topham Picturepoint/Topfoto.co.uk, left, ©Cambridgeshire Collection; p.75 Top left, bottom, ©Cambridgeshire Collection, top right, ©Reproduced with the permission of

the Provost and Scholars of King's College, Cambridge. Ref:RCB/Ph/262, held in library; p.76 Top, Centre, Bottom, ©Cambridgeshire Collection; p.77 Top right, ©Cambridgeshire Collection, bottom, ©Bertrand Russell Archives, McMaster University Library, Canada; p.78 Top right, centre right & bottom right, ©The Cambridge Collection; p.79 Top & bottom ©Cambridgeshire Collection; p.80 Centre left, ©Popperfoto/alamy.com, centre right, ©Reuters/Corbis, bottom, ©Cambridgeshire Collection; p.81 Bottom left, ©Hulton-Deutsch Collection/Corbis, bottom right, ©Bettmann/Corbis, centre left & centre right, ©Hart McLeod; p.82 Top, bottom, ©Cambridgeshire Collection; p.83 Top & bottom, ©Cambridgeshire Collection; p.84 Top & bottom, ©Hart McLeod; p.85 Top left, ©The Cavendish Laboratory, University of Cambridge, top right, ©Reproduced by kind permission of the Cambridge Evening News, bottom, ©Hart McLeod; p.86 Bottom, ©Reproduced by kind permission of the Cambridge Evening News, top & centre, ©Hart McLeod; p.87, Bottom left, ©Reproduced by kind permission of the Cambridge Evening News, top & bottom right ©Hart McLeod; p.88 Top right, ©Hart McLeod, centre, ©Cambridgeshire Collection; p.89 Top right & bottom left, © Richard Summers, Wellcome Trust Sanger Institute; p.90 Top, ©R. Williams (STScI), the Hubble Deep Field Team and NASA, bottom right, ©Department of Mathematical and Theoretical Physics, University of Cambridge, bottom left, © Reproduced by kind permission of the Cambridge Evening News; p.91 Top Right, ©Hulton-Deutsch Collection/Corbis, Bottom, ©Gregory Pace/Corbis, centre right, ©Rex Features; p.92 Top, centre, bottom left & bottom right, ©Hart McLeod; p.93 Bottom right, © Reproduced by kind permission of the Cambridge Evening News, top right & bottom right, ©Hart McLeod; p.94 Top & bottom right, ©Cambridgeshire Collection; p.95 Top, ©Cambridgeshire Collection, centre & bottom, ©Hart McLeod.

Particular thanks also to Mike Petty, and Chris Jakes at the Cambridgeshire Collection.

Title page pictures:
Cambridge from prehistoric times to the present day:
(top left) The site of the iron-age hill fort at Wandlebury, seen from the air.
(below) The medieval chapel at King's College
(right) The Microsoft Research Laboratory in Cambridge. It was funded by Bill Gates who has also provided more than 200 scholarships to Cambridge. This building on the West Cambridge University site, named after the mathematician, Roger Needham, was completed in 2001.

Text Acknowledgements:
p.67 Grantchester Meadows written by, Roger Waters, ©Lupus Music Co Ltd.

Apologies to anyone who may have been inadvertently missed from this list. The Publisher has made every effort to trace the copyright holders of material used in this book. Any omissions will be rectified in subsequent printings if information is passed to the Publisher.

Many thanks to the following for all their help and support:
Richard Fisher, Ally Large, Philippa O'Neill,
Emma Rhind-Tutt and Paul Stelmaszczyk.

Contents

Cambridge: a famous city

Cambridge is a small city on the edge of the Fens, yet is famous throughout the world. Why is this so?

A world-class university

Cambridge is best known for its ancient university, which ranks as one of the top universities in the world.

Cambridge University has produced some of the greatest scientists, mathematicians, writers and thinkers of their times and continues to attract many brilliant people. The Nobel Prize, probably the most sought-after prize in the world, has been won by Cambridge graduates 80 times since it began in 1901.

From market town to hi-tech city

Although Cambridge owes its present fame to the University, it first thrived in Roman times as a small riverside settlement. By medieval times it was a busy town and inland port, best known for hosting the famous Stourbridge Fair, one of the largest fairs in Europe. More recently, Cambridge has become famous for its science industry. Its phenomenal growth has become known as the 'Cambridge Phenomenon'.

Cambridge City shield, Guildhall. The river, bridge and castle are important features on the shield. King John first granted the town a royal charter in 1201. In 1951, Cambridge became a city.

Beautiful buildings and landscapes

Cambridge is also famous for some of the most superb architecture and landscaping in the world. There are many stunning college buildings, such as King's College Chapel and the Wren Library at Trinity, which back onto idyllic stretches of water (the Backs).

Punting on the Backs, beneath the Bridge of Sighs, St John's College.

The historic heart of Cambridge. This picture shows many of the colleges, with the River Cam to the left.

Cambridge and the Fens

The Fens were once a flooded and marshy landscape, dotted with islands where settlements such as Ely grew up. Cambridge sat on the fen-edge. Since the 17th century the fenland has been drained, making it now one of the richest farming areas in the country.

Cambridge has been closely linked to the Fens through many centuries of river trade. Goods were transported by boat to and from Cambridge via the large seaport of King's Lynn. Cambridge still has special links with Ely, its cathedral town since 1109.

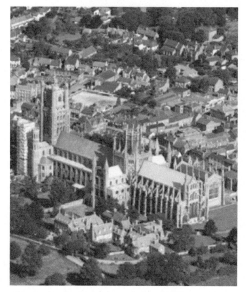

Ely Cathedral. The cathedral is known as the 'Ship of the Fens' because its distinctive shape dominates the fen landscape for miles around.

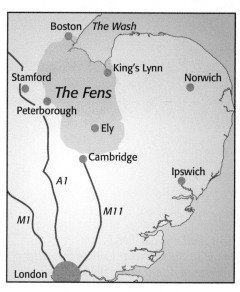

Cambridge sits on the edge of the Fens. Today, the Fens are a vast expanse of very flat, low-lying land that stretches northwards as far as the Wash.

1 Prehistoric times

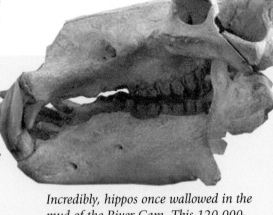

The earliest human remains in the Cambridge area have been found along the River Cam, or Cam Valley. This was where stone-age people could best survive. They moved from place to place, living in temporary camps and looking for food along the fertile river valley. The first proper settlement that we can consider 'Cambridge' was an iron-age village on Castle Hill. This was settled by Celts in about 500 BC.

Incredibly, hippos once wallowed in the mud of the River Cam. This 120,000-year-old skeleton was discovered in the ancient river bed at Barrington, just outside Cambridge.

The Stone Age (500000 – 3000 BC)

The climate in Britain during the Stone Age went through many changes, varying from sub-tropical to glacial. Early people survived by hunting animals and fish with basic stone tools, and gathering food from the forest.

In the local area, the earliest people settled in the Cam Valley, an excellent place for hunting and gathering food. The river flowed through a wide valley where large animals such as oxen roamed, and smaller animals such as wild pigs and deer lived in the nearby forest. The forest was also abundant with fruits, roots and nuts, whilst the river and marshes provided a plentiful supply of fish and fowl.

Some of the oldest finds in the Cambridge area have been found on Castle Hill. Hundreds of flint hand-axes were discovered near Huntingdon Road, dating from at least 210000 BC.

The Cam Valley: hot spot

The wildlife living along the River Cam was once very different from today. Stone-age fossils and bones which have been dug from the original river bed include those of hippos, rhinos, lions, elephants and hyenas. Nowadays these animals live in savannah and wetlands areas of Africa.

The first farmers: Neolithic times (3000 – 2000 BC)

A tremendous change happened about 5,000 years ago when people in Europe first started farming. Neolithic people – as the early farmers are known – began to keep animals such as pigs and goats, and grow crops including wheat and barley.

The Cam Valley was a good, fertile place for farming. Neolithic people living there grew crops and also continued to hunt and gather resources from fen, river valley and forest. Although they could now settle in one place for longer, they still moved on from time to time, clearing new land as they went. Families lived in small, shifting settlements of about three to six houses, every few miles along the river valley.

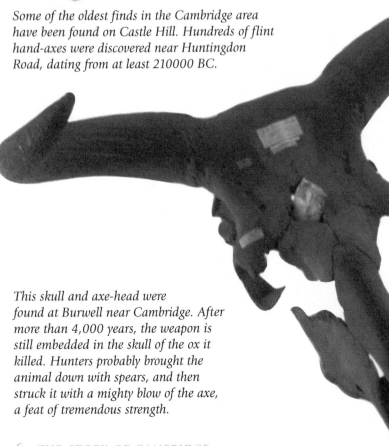

This skull and axe-head were found at Burwell near Cambridge. After more than 4,000 years, the weapon is still embedded in the skull of the ox it killed. Hunters probably brought the animal down with spears, and then struck it with a mighty blow of the axe, a feat of tremendous strength.

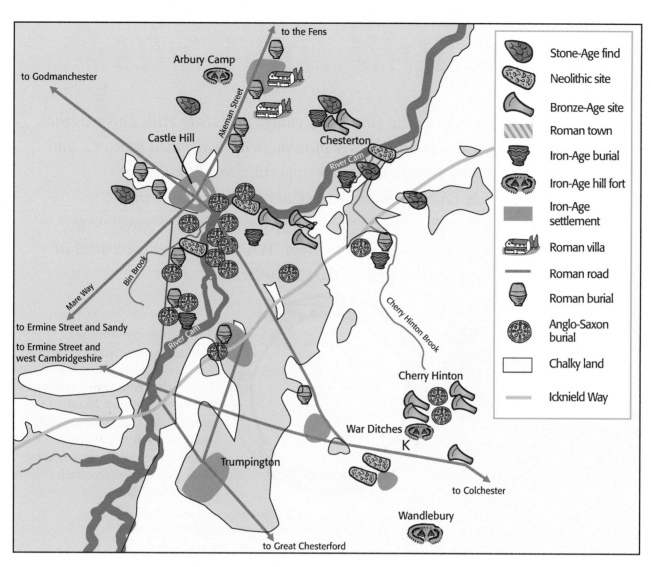

Map legend:
- Stone-Age find
- Neolithic site
- Bronze-Age site
- Roman town
- Iron-Age burial
- Iron-Age hill fort
- Iron-Age settlement
- Roman villa
- Roman road
- Roman burial
- Anglo-Saxon burial
- Chalky land
- Icknield Way

Map labels: to the Fens, to Godmanchester, Arbury Camp, Akeman Street, Castle Hill, River Cam, Chesterton, Bin Brook, Mare Way, to Ermine Street and Sandy, to Ermine Street and west Cambridgeshire, River Cam, Cherry Hinton Brook, Cherry Hinton, War Ditches, K, Trumpington, to Colchester, Wandlebury, to Great Chesterford

The Cam Valley. There have been many prehistoric finds along the River Cam, as this map shows. When bronze- and iron-age people built more permanent homes, they settled on the chalky land which was easier to farm.

The first metal-users: the Bronze Age (2000 – 700 BC)

During the Bronze Age, bronze became the most commonly worked metal, used for tools and weapons. In the local area, bronze-age people continued to live and farm along the river valley and on the drier, fertile chalklands. They now also began to live in more permanent settlements.

Fierce tribal warfare was a feature of life about 3,000 years ago. Near Cambridge, the bronze-age tribes built large earth and timber fortifications, including War Ditches (later an iron-age hill fort) at Cherry Hinton.

A rare find: a beautifully decorated bronze-age beaker, from about 1600 BC. It was found in a round barrow (burial chamber) at Little Downham.

Cambridge in the Iron Age (700 BC – AD 43)

Over 2,500 years ago, iron was widely used for the first time. The early iron-users were Celts. They originally migrated to Britain from northern Europe.

Many Celts settled along the Cam Valley, either in farmsteads (consisting of a few round houses, fields and paddocks), or clustered in small villages. Archaeologists have unearthed the remains of some larger villages in the area too, including Trumpington, Grantchester, Abington, Linton, and one on Castle Hill (which later became modern-day Cambridge).

The Celts left their mark prominently on the local landscape. They constructed large, circular hill forts at sites such as Wandlebury (see page 9), to defend themselves from neighbouring Celtic tribes.

An iron sickle from the 1st century BC. Farming improved with the new iron-tipped tools.

Cambridge and the Celts

In the 1st century BC there was a large Celtic (iron-age) village on Castle Hill. This was the first true settlement of Cambridge. It was on the edge of some fiercely disputed territory, and because of its frontier location, Castle Hill grew into an important local settlement.

The three main warring tribes in East Anglia were the Catuvellauni (based in Hertfordshire), the Trinovantes (from Essex) and the Iceni (from Norfolk). From time to time, the village on Castle Hill was overrun by enemy tribes. When the Romans invaded in the 1st century AD, Castle Hill was in the hands of the Catuvellauni.

The first settlement of Cambridge

On Castle Hill, the combination of river, fen and hillside made it a perfect site for survival and defence. The village was densely inhabited and defended with ditches. There were other Celtic settlements close by, some only recently discovered. These include a large village near Huntingdon Road, one near Arbury Road and another on Newmarket Road.

The Celts built their houses from wattle and daub (a frame of branches interwoven with twigs and plastered with a mixture of clay, lime and water). Each family dwelling was home to as many as 15 to 20 people.

Celtic warriors

The Celts were famous throughout the Roman Empire for their warlike character. In battle, they must have appeared wild and terrifying, daubed in woad (blue dye) and wielding their iron swords. Warrior chiefs were highly respected by their people and received special burials.

The richest burial in the Cambridge area was discovered at Newnham Croft. Here, a warrior chief from the 3rd century BC was found buried with his most valued possessions, including this fine brooch and decorated bronze bracelet.

Castle Hill in the 1st century AD.

This bronze mirror was found at Great Chesterford near Cambridge. The front of the mirror would have been highly polished to give a reflection. The swirling pattern is a typical Celtic design.

Wandlebury today. This was once an iron-age hill fort. The circular ditch can be seen clearly from the air. The Celts lived in houses within the perimeter of the ditch.

Celtic hill forts

The Celts built many impressive fortifications on hilltops, large enough to accommodate scores of people and hundreds of animals. There were three hill forts in the Cambridge area (see map on page 7). The most important one was at Wandlebury.

Today, Wandlebury is a peaceful country park and a wonderful haven for wildlife. Over 2,000 years ago, it was a Catuvellauni hill fort and the scene of some savage hand-to-hand fighting. The fortifications were built in a key strategic position: on the crest of the chalk hills south of Cambridge – the Gog Magog Hills – overlooking the whole Cam Valley and the ancient Icknield Way. (The Icknield Way is one of the oldest roads in England, running along a long ridge of chalk hills, but now just a track remains.) From here, the Catuvellauni had a commanding view over their Iceni and Trinovantes neighbours.

The Gog Magog Hills

Rising to a height of just 71 metres above sea level, these gently rolling hills are one of the highest points in Cambridgeshire. The hills were named after two terrible giants, Gog and Magog. According to legend, they were the last survivors of a race of giants who used to live in Britain. Some archaeologists believed until recently that an ancient figure of Gog was once cut out of white chalk on the hills, where it could be seen for miles around.

The original circular ditch was over four metres deep. The soil from the ditch was used to build an inner rampart nearly five metres high, supported with wooden posts, and with a palisade (strong fencing) on top. It would have been very hard to attack. Assailants would have had to struggle uphill, armed with heavy swords, shields and spears, as well as slingshots and ammunition, to face a deep ditch and a towering embankment of earth. All the while, the defending warriors would be firing a barrage of missiles, such as rocks and heavy logs, from the palisade above.

In the 18th century, Lord Godolphin built a large country house on the site. Many of the ditches were filled in to make landscaped gardens. Much prehistoric evidence was disturbed or lost forever.

2 Invaders and settlers

From the 1st century AD, Britain was raided, invaded and settled by many different people. The invasions continued for the next 1,000 years. The Romans invaded from Italy, the Anglo-Saxons from north Germany, the Vikings and Danes from Scandinavia and the Normans from northern France. They all had an enduring effect on the country, and on the small riverside town of Cambridge.

The Roman invaders

In AD 43, the Emperor Claudius sent 20,000 legionaries to invade Britain. For the next 400 years, the country was ruled from Rome, and Cambridge became a small Roman town in a vast Roman Empire. By the 5th century, the Roman Empire started to fall apart. The Roman soldiers went home, abandoning Britain, and leaving the Romano-British people (by now a mixture of Romans and Celts) to live in the crumbling walled town of Cambridge.

Roman invaders on the march. The Romans needed good, straight roads for their soldiers to march quickly from place to place.

Long straight roads like this one (the old Roman Akeman Street) are a lasting reminder that the Romans once occupied Cambridge.

Anglo-Saxon invaders

From about AD 400, Anglo-Saxon tribes from north Germany and Denmark arrived on English shores. At first, they raided the countryside but soon they settled and became peaceful farmers. In Anglo-Saxon times, Cambridge grew and expanded southwards across the river, from its original site on Castle Hill (see map on page 17, bottom).

The Anglo-Saxons crossed the North Sea in long wooden boats. They reached Cambridge by rowing up the Rivers Great Ouse and Cam from the Wash (see map opposite).

An Anglo-Saxon pot from about AD 400.

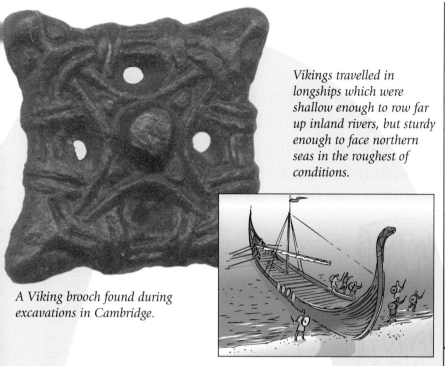

A Viking brooch found during excavations in Cambridge.

Vikings travelled in longships which were shallow enough to row far up inland rivers, but sturdy enough to face northern seas in the roughest of conditions.

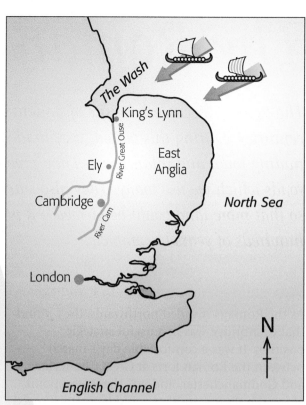

Viking and Danish invaders

During the 9th century, Vikings from Scandinavia and Danes from Denmark raided the British coastline. In 865, hordes of Danes reached Mercia (the Midlands) and East Anglia. They plundered and destroyed Anglo-Saxon monasteries, including that at nearby Ely. In 875, a huge Danish army reached Cambridge, led by a chief called Guthrum.

The Saxons fought back. Alfred the Great, King of Wessex, and his army stopped the Danes taking over the whole of England. The Danes agreed to stay in an area of England known as the 'Danelaw', where English and Danes were equal in law (see map on page 17, top). Cambridge stayed under Danish control for about 50 years.

Finally the Saxons won back England, and the town became Saxon once more.

The Normans crossed the English Channel with a fleet of ships loaded with knights, archers and horses. This scene from the Bayeux Tapestry shows the Normans conquering Hastings

Norman invaders

In the late 11th century there was a new threat from across the Channel when the Normans claimed the English throne. In 1066, William the Conqueror won the Battle of Hastings and was proclaimed King of England. He and his army finally reached Cambridge in 1068, building a castle to make the Norman victory secure.

1,000 years of invasions
The Cambridge area has always been open to invaders from the sea. They could travel up the rivers of East Anglia by boat, deep into the region, quickly reaching settlements such as Cambridge.

Doorway of the Leper Hospital at Barnwell, Cambridge, built shortly after the Norman Conquest. Lepers who were ravaged by disease would come to pray in this simple 12th-century chapel. (See also page 21.)

The Roman invaders

The Romans occupied the site of present-day Cambridge for about four centuries. During this period, they made Cambridge into a sizeable trading town and inland port. They gave Cambridge many of the main roads which we use today. They also started draining the marshy fenland so that more land could be farmed – a process which was to take many hundreds of years to complete.

Why build a military camp in Cambridge?

As the Romans invaded northwards, they found that Cambridge was in a useful strategic position. It was a comfortable day's march between the Roman forts at Great Chesterford and Godmanchester, and was the lowest point along the River Cam that could be easily crossed (see map on page 7). The site was also convenient for river transport, and commanded a main route into Britain from the North Sea.

Inhabitants of Castle Hill today are living on the site of the original Roman fort and walled town.

The Romans originally built many of the main roads still used in the city today, such as Huntingdon Road and Hills Road. This 4th-century Roman milestone was found near Girton.

A Roman camp on Castle Hill

The first Roman invaders set up a military camp on Castle Hill in AD 43. At first, it was more like an army staging post than a fully fledged Roman town. No families lived on the site until a century later.

In AD 60, the Romans faced their most serious threat. Queen Boudica and the Iceni tribe led a rebellion against their hated enemy. Boudica was a powerful local leader. The Roman historian, Cassius Dio, described her like this:

> In stature she was very tall, in appearance most terrifying, in the glance of her eye most fierce, and her voice was harsh; a great mass of red hair fell to her hips...

The Romans were completely unprepared. Although the rebellion had centred on Colchester, the Romans hastily improved their defences in Cambridge. They built a large wooden fort surrounded by ditches, near where Shire Hall now stands.

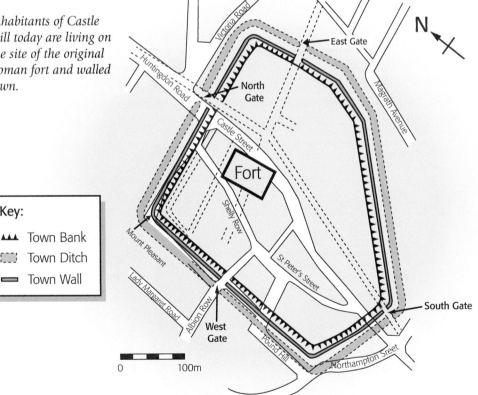

Key:
- ▲▲▲ Town Bank
- ▭▭▭ Town Ditch
- ▬▬▬ Town Wall

0   100m

Plan of Roman Cambridge. There was a gate into the Roman camp near where Albion Row now meets Mount Pleasant. Nearly 2,000 years ago, Roman soldiers would have marched through here on their way to the barracks, their iron-studded sandals echoing on the cobbled paving.

These skeletons were discovered in the basement of houses during recent building work in Jesus Lane. Archaeologists investigated the site and revealed an ancient Roman burial ground just outside the Roman settlement of Cambridge.

Cambridge becomes a walled town

About 100 years after the Romans had arrived, the immediate military threat was over. The Romans now replaced their army camp with a small town. It was appropriately named *Duroliponte* – 'town by the boggy river'. The Romans laid out the streets in a regular grid pattern, lined with rectangular houses built of timber, wattle and daub.

In the 4th century, the Romans needed to improve their defences because of a new danger: this time the Anglo-Saxons. The Romans built stronger walls, fortified gates and watchtowers around Cambridge. This gave it status as a proper Roman town.

Local hero: Queen Boudica

Boudica was the warrior queen of the Iceni tribe of Norfolk. Outraged by the Romans' bullying behaviour, she led a successful attack against the enemy. It sent shockwaves throughout the Roman Empire. Leading 80,000 Iceni rebels, Boudica marched from Thetford to Colchester, passing close by the military camp at Cambridge.

Boudica and the rebels burned Colchester, London and St Albans to the ground. They massacred the Romans mercilessly, soldiers and civilians alike. Finally there was a showdown between the Celts and Romans in the Midlands. The Roman army won decisively.

The cause of Boudica's death is unknown, but according to modern myth, her body lies buried beneath Platforms 10 and 11 of London's King's Cross Station.

A Roman villa

Outside the town there were many Roman villas – large country houses with farms attached. The villa in Arbury was one of the closest ones to Cambridge. It was excavated in the 1950s when new houses were built on what had previously been open fields.

Romans lived here from about AD 130 to 400. The villa was built out of stone with a tiled roof, the inside walls were plastered and brightly painted, and there were glass windows. The ultimate in 4th-century luxury – especially for a Roman living through the cold, damp Cambridge winter – was a hypocaust (underfloor heating).

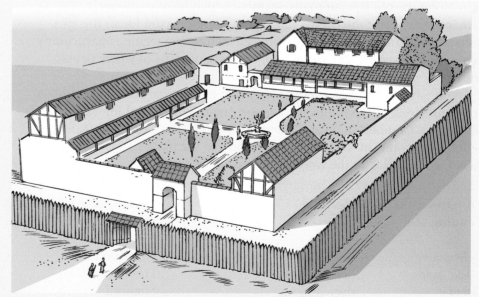

The Roman villa in Arbury. What is now an area covered with houses was once the site of a single luxury Roman villa set in seven acres of farmland.

The first Anglo-Saxon settlers

As the Roman Empire collapsed, the Roman legions finally left Britain. From AD 410, the people left living in the walled town of Cambridge had to fend for themselves against attacks from foreign invaders. The Anglo-Saxons were particularly attracted to the fertile land of the Cam Valley where they settled in scattered villages and hamlets. The town of Cambridge itself was largely abandoned, and it became a quiet backwater for the next few hundred years.

This beautiful Anglo-Saxon gold brooch is studded with precious stones. It was found at Barrington cemetery near Cambridge. Brooches were decorative but also important for fastening woollen clothing.

Early Anglo-Saxon Cambridge

From the 5th to 7th centuries, Cambridge declined as a town. Although some Anglo-Saxons did settle in the Roman town on Castle Hill, they may have found it already virtually deserted. In 695, Cambridge was still a remote place, described by the monk and scholar, St Bede, as 'a little ruined city'. It was not until the 8th century that Cambridge grew and flourished once more. The Anglo-Saxons aptly named their small Cambridge settlement *Grantacaestir*, or 'the Roman fort by the Granta'. The word *Granta* meant 'muddy river'.

Settlers in the Cam Valley

From the 5th century, most Anglo-Saxons settled in the river valleys, rather than along the old Roman roads, many of which fell into disuse. Archaeologists have discovered much about Anglo-Saxon life in the area from the remains of houses and from cemeteries. The region is particularly rich in Anglo-Saxon place names too, showing patterns of where people settled.

Anglo-Saxons used place names to describe where particular individuals or groups lived. For example, *ton* was the Anglo-Saxon word for 'farm' or 'village', so Comberton meant 'Cumbra's village'. The word *ing* meant 'the people of'; *ley* meant 'clearing in the wood'; so the place name Madingley meant 'the clearing in the wood of the people of Mada'.

Early Anglo-Saxon houses were built of wood with thatched roofs like this.

Burying the dead

It was the pagan custom to bury the dead with their most valuable possessions, such as weapons and jewellery. Many Anglo-Saxon cemeteries have been discovered in Cambridge and the surrounding area. The largest one is under St John's College Cricket Field.

Recently, there was a particularly exciting excavation at Barrington. Archaeologists found the remains of 43 Anglo-Saxons, dating from the 6th to 7th centuries. Most of these people died before the age of 40. The bones suggest that they ate healthily, and were about the same height that we are today.

Anglo-Saxon ending	Meaning	Local village with this ending
-den, dene	valley	Great Eversden
-feld, field	field	Haslingfield
-ford	river crossing	Shelford
-ham	settlement	Newnham
-worth	land with a hedge around it	Boxworth

The mystery of Devil's Dyke

Devil's Dyke is a remarkable Anglo-Saxon ditch and rampart near Cambridge. It stretches for over eight miles in a straight line, like a scar across the flat, low-lying countryside. At present, the ditch is nearly 5 metres deep, but 15 centuries ago it would certainly have been deeper. In a tremendous feat of engineering, the Anglo-Saxons excavated millions of tons of earth and chalk using just basic hand tools.

The purpose of the ditch has baffled archaeologists. Some think that the East Anglian Saxons built it to block attacks from the Mercian tribes to the west (see map on page 16).

According to myth, Devil's Dyke was not dug at all, but was the work of the devil. When he discovered that he had not been invited to a local wedding, the devil rushed angrily across East Anglia, flicking his tail and so etching the ditch onto the landscape.

An extremely rare discovery at Barrington: the bed-burial of a woman. This is how she may have looked at her burial. Laid upon her body were a pouch containing magical amulets and a weaving baton in the shape of a sword. The woman is lying on a bed, showing that she was an important person in her community, possibly a healer or storyteller.

Saxon and Viking town

In the 7th and 8th centuries, England was divided into seven Anglo-Saxon kingdoms. At first, Cambridge was in the kingdom of East Anglia, but in the 8th century, Mercia (the Midlands) became very powerful under King Offa. He conquered large parts of East Anglia, and the town now came under Mercian rule.

However, the region remained at risk of attack. In the 9th century, invaders from northern Europe raided the coast, sweeping up the fenland rivers in their large, oared ships. This time, the attackers were Danes, or Vikings. Finally, in the 10th century, the Anglo-Saxons won back control of Cambridge.

Coin minted in the time of King Offa. He ruled over Cambridge in the late 8th century.

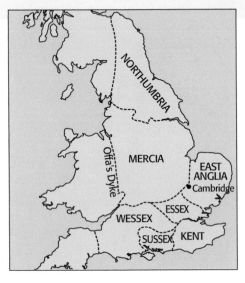

Anglo-Saxon kingdoms in the 7th century. The map shows Cambridge as an important border town between the great kingdoms of Mercia and East Anglia. The River Cam acted as part of the boundary between the two kingdoms.

Cambridge under King Offa

King Offa's kingdom of Mercia was so vast that it stretched from Offa's Dyke on the Welsh border right across to Cambridge. Offa made his Cambridge base on Castle Hill, and re-used the ancient Roman walls to build a strong, well-defended town. He obviously felt safe from attack, for he ordered a wooden bridge to be built across the river. The bridge was so important that it became known simply as Great Bridge and the town took on a new name, *Grantabrycge*. River trade flourished once more.

The town spreads south

Cambridge had been a settlement on the north side of the river for hundreds of years. But from the 8th century, the Anglo-Saxons began to settle on the south side too. The land on this bank was more waterlogged, so the Anglo-Saxons built their houses on hillocks where the ground was less likely to flood. This higher ground included Market Hill and Peas Hill. The hills are scarcely noticeable today because the ground has been levelled gradually over many centuries, but they are still referred to in our modern street names.

By late Saxon times, the town had shifted dramatically southwards from the original Roman settlement. In the 10th century, King's Parade and Trumpington Street effectively formed the town's high street (see opposite).

How Cambridge got its name

Cambridge is named after the wooden bridge that once crossed the Cam (very close to where Magdalene Bridge is today). The town's name has changed gradually over time:

- In the 7th century, the town was called *Grantacaestir*; –caestir referred to the Roman fort on Castle Hill.
- In the 8th century, the town became known as *Grantabrycge*; –brycge referred to the Anglo-Saxon bridge over the Cam. The bridge, rather than the fort, had now become the notable feature of the town.
- By 1300, the name had changed to *Cambrigge*.
- By 1600, the name *Cambridge* was commonly used.

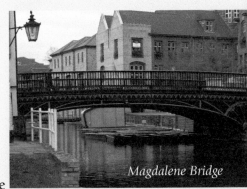

Magdalene Bridge

Viking raiders and traders

In 875, an army of Vikings reached Cambridge and the Saxons were forced to surrender. Cambridge became part of a large Danish territory called the Danelaw. By the 9th century the Vikings had become Christians. They built their town on the south side of the river, by Great Bridge.

In the heart of what was once Viking Cambridge, St Clement's Church still stands (on Bridge Street). St Clement was a popular saint of Danish sailors. The present church dates from medieval times, but its name and location near the river suggest that this was originally a Viking church.

▲ *East Anglia under Danelaw.*

The Vikings lived up to their reputation as great international traders. They came from as far away as Dublin and Cork, travelling up the River Cam, bringing goods such as Irish woollen cloth into Cambridge, where it was unloaded at Quayside.

Late Saxon Cambridge

In 917, Cambridge became a Saxon town, now ruled by King Edward the Elder (son of Alfred the Great). He marked out the town with a defensive ditch later known as the King's Ditch and this became the town boundary for many hundreds of years (see also map on page 21). By late Saxon times, Cambridge was a thriving town with a busy market place (still in the same position today), numerous churches, watermills by the river, its own law court and a mint where silver coins were made.

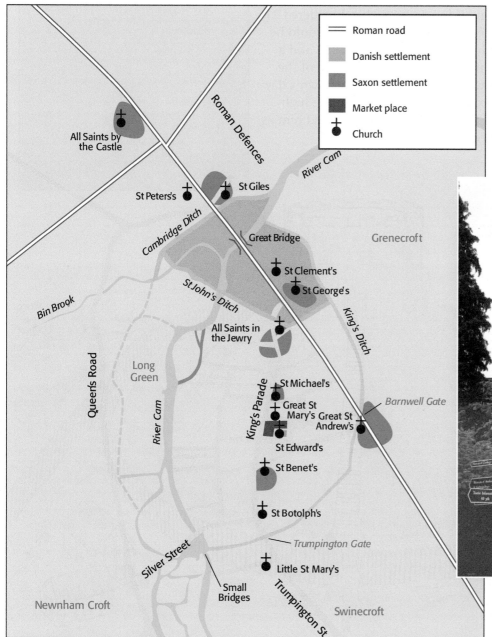

Late Saxon Cambridge

The Saxon tower of St Benedict's Church (St Bene't's for short) is the oldest surviving building in the town, built in about 1000.

The Norman Conquest

The Normans reached Cambridge in 1068, two years after defeating Harold at the Battle of Hastings. King William seized control of the town and ordered a castle to be built. Today, a great earth mound on Castle Hill is the only visible reminder of the Normans' rule.

It took William five years to bring England under his control. The very last pocket of resistance in the country was in the Fens just north of Cambridge. Here, the local Saxon rebel, Hereward the Wake, held out against the Normans until 1072.

The Normans invade

When William I and his army reached Cambridge, he immediately ordered 27 Saxon houses to be ripped down on Castle Hill so that a large castle could be built there. The castle consisted of a massive earth mound (the *motte*) and a wooden enclosure (the *bailey*). It became the home and military base of the first Norman sheriff of the county, Picot, who was in charge of the town's day-to-day running. Picot was hated by the Saxons, especially for extorting high taxes. His reputation quickly spread. The Saxon monks at Ely described him as 'a hungry lion, a ravening wolf, a filthy hog'.

This mound is all that now remains of William the Conqueror's castle.

The Norman castle probably looked like this. It showed the Saxons that the Normans were now firmly in power.

Hereward the Wake: rebel of the Fens

In 1068, King William faced one of his toughest challenges when Hereward and his band of Saxon rebels made a last stand against the Normans at Ely.

William was determined to crush Hereward and take control of Ely (an island in those days) and the surrounding Fens. Setting out from Cambridge castle, his army built a causeway across the marshes using bundles of wood and stone. As his men crossed it, the causeway collapsed and many Norman soldiers drowned in the marshes. Undeterred, the Normans built a second causeway. But the Saxons had the advantage of local knowledge of the Fens. They threw oil onto the reeds and set fire to the thick vegetation. Many hundreds of Normans were burned to death.

Finally, William built a castle at Wisbech. He cleverly besieged the rebels, cutting off their food supply from the Wash. According to local legend, as the rebels grew more desperate, Hereward was betrayed by some Saxon monks, and the Normans were secretly shown a route across the Fens. Hereward managed to escape but the revolt was finally crushed.

Hereward the Wake captured the imagination of many Victorian writers such as the great Cambridge historian, Charles Kingsley. Hereward was portrayed as a national Saxon hero, fighting against the cruel Norman invaders. The truth may have been rather different. He was a well-known mercenary who had earlier been banished from home by his own father.

The Isle of Ely was once the site of one of the richest and most famous Saxon monasteries in the land. It was run by the Abbot of Ely, a very powerful man in the region. A splendid cathedral was built in Ely by the Normans on the site of the original monastery church. Ely officially became a cathedral town in 1109, and Cambridge became part of its diocese.

New churches and monasteries

After the invasion, the Normans built many new churches and monasteries. In 1092, Sheriff Picot ordered a church to be built at St Giles, next to the castle where he lived. Picot also set up the first monastery in Cambridge, a house for six monks, next to St Giles. In 1112, it moved to some common land near Barnwell, where there was a holy well. From these humble beginnings grew the largest and most lavish monastery in Cambridge: Barnwell Priory (see page 25). The best-known Norman building in Cambridge is the Church of the Holy Sepulchre, or Round Church, which was built in 1101.

The Round Church with its distinctive Norman pillars.

3 Medieval Cambridge

In medieval times, Cambridge was a thriving market town and inland port, defended by a castle. The town also had its own law courts and elected mayor. These were great privileges granted by the King.

Cambridge might have remained a prosperous yet modest town, but for the chance arrival of some scholars fleeing from Oxford in 1209. They were to change the town for ever: Cambridge was to become a leading university town in Europe.

The castle
Edward I rebuilt the town's wooden castle in stone, which was imported by river at vast expense. The castle probably looked like this.

The oldest house in Cambridge
This house, known today as the School of Pythagorus, was built in about 1200. It probably belonged to a wealthy merchant as it was built of stone and was located near the quayside, the hub of Cambridge trading. It must have stood out from the shamble of thatched, timber-framed houses that most townspeople lived in.

Peterhouse: the first college
In the early 13th century, the new university changed the face of the medieval town. At first, most students lived in hostels. Later in the century, the first colleges were built. Peterhouse, shown here, is the oldest and smallest college in Cambridge.

Defending the town

In medieval times, Cambridge was often raided by rebels and outlaws, especially from the Fens to the north. During King Stephen's reign, Cambridge suffered at the hands of a particularly troublesome baron, Geoffrey de Mandeville, who made his base in Ely. From there, he attacked and plundered many fen-edge towns, including Cambridge, with his own private army.

The castle was key to Cambridge's defences. The original Norman castle was rebuilt in stone in the 13th century to make it stronger.

Some medieval towns, such as Oxford, were also defended with formidable stone walls. Cambridge, instead, had a combination of natural and man-made defences, forming a 'wall of water' around the town. The town was completely encircled by the River Cam, which flowed from south to north, and the King's Ditch (see map).

The Leper Hospital

In medieval times, leprosy was rife and lepers were treated as outcasts. People were terrified of coming into contact with the infectious and disabling disease. This tiny chapel on Barnwell Road is all that remains of the Leper Hospital of St Mary Magdalene, built in the early 12th century. At that time, this would have been a remote spot, far from the town boundary.

Monks and nuns

Religious houses such as the Priory of St Radegund (now part of Jesus College) were built in isolated places so that the monks and nuns would be cut off from worldly distractions and live simpler lives, dedicated to God. This picture, taken from the brook that once skirted the nunnery, conveys a feeling of seclusion that the medieval convent must once have had.

The Black Death strikes

Whilst most parts of Cambridge grew in medieval times, a few areas declined. The parish of All-Saints-by-the-Castle disappeared completely in the mid-14th century when the deadly plague struck, wiping out nearly the whole community.

The King's Ditch

This ditch, first built for defence, soon attracted people's rubbish, slops and sewage, as well as waste and carcasses from the nearby slaughter houses. Living near the King's Ditch in the height of summer could not have been pleasant or healthy!

The Town Gates

To enter the town from the south, people had to pass through the large wooden gates that spanned the road at either Trumpington or Barnwell Gate.

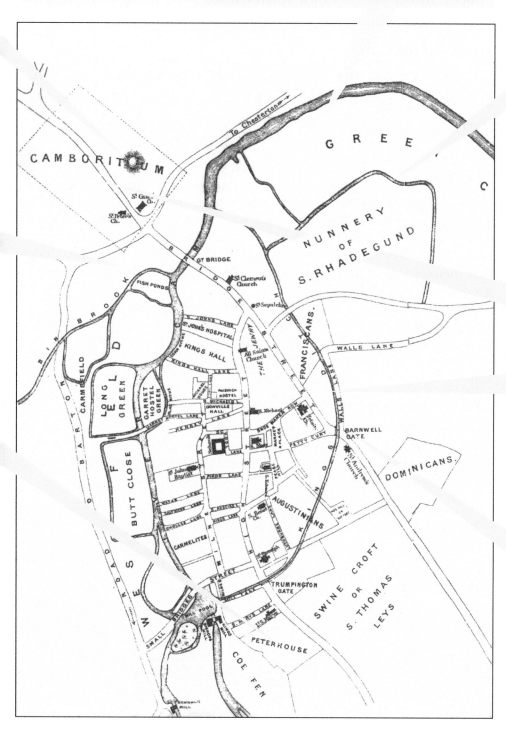

Map showing Cambridge in the 14th century. Compared with today, the medieval town was much smaller. The King's Ditch – the town boundary then – would have excluded most of what we regard as the modern city.

River trade, markets and fairs

Newnham Mill today. Corn was first milled here in 1550. It has now been converted into a restaurant, complete with water wheel!

Cambridge has been an important trading centre for hundreds of years. In medieval times, much local produce was traded here, including fish, eels and sedge (a thick grass for thatching) from the Fens to the north, and wheat and barley from the rich arable land to the south. Most goods were transported in and out of Cambridge by boat. Many people in the town earned their living from the river trade, either as merchants, or as boatmen plying their barges up and down the Cam.

Cambridge was also the site of a vast international trade fair, Stourbridge Fair, on the banks of the River Cam. The annual fair started in the 13th century and continued for over 700 years.

Cambridge: a wealthy port

In the early 12th century, King Henry I issued a writ making Cambridge the chief port in the shire (county). This meant that the town had a monopoly of local river trade, and grew at the expense of other towns further downstream.

The main commercial area of Cambridge was Quayside, near Magdalene Bridge, or Great Bridge (see map on page 21). There were other quays lining the river where the lawns of King's College, Trinity and St John's now stretch. As the colleges grew, in the 15th and 16th centuries, nearly all of these were swept away. Trading was now concentrated at each end of the Backs – Quayside and the Mill Pool.

At the Mill Pool, corn was ground into flour at one of the town's three main mills. These included the King's Mill (built by the first Norman sheriff, Picot), and another ancient mill next door, Bishop's Mill. Both of these mills competed fiercely with Newnham Mill, a short distance upstream.

The Market Place

In medieval times, the market spread over a much larger area than it does today. Old street names give clues about what was sold in the different parts. Like a modern-day assembly line, animals were slaughtered and butchered in connecting streets, Slaughter House Lane and Butcher Street. The animal hides were then sold on to Shoemaker Row, where they were made into leather goods.

Vegetables, milk and butter were sold by the market cross. The fish market was on Peas Hill (near the Arts' Theatre). The name *Petty Cury* meant 'Little Cookery'. It was once a main thoroughfare lined with pastry cooks' stalls. *Petty*, meaning *petit*, or small, distinguished it from the main Cook's Row on Market Hill.

Present-day street name	Medieval name
Guildhall Street	Butcher Street
Wheeler Street	Short Butcher Row
Market Street	Shoemaker Row or Cordwainer Street
Corn Exchange Street	Slaughter House Lane

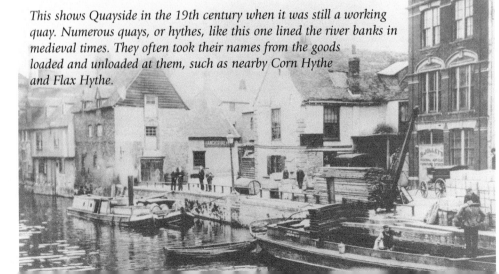

This shows Quayside in the 19th century when it was still a working quay. Numerous quays, or hythes, like this one lined the river banks in medieval times. They often took their names from the goods loaded and unloaded at them, such as nearby Corn Hythe and Flax Hythe.

Stourbridge Fair

This fair was held on Stourbridge Common, near the Hospital of St Mary Magdalene (see picture on page 21). Traders brought a huge variety of goods by barge or packhorse from miles around, including woollen cloth from Suffolk and Yorkshire; tin from Cornwall; lead from Derbyshire; and oysters from Colchester. Imported luxuries included wine from France, silks from Italy and furs from the Baltic.

The fair opened each year after the harvest, in September. For a whole month, the rows of booths heaved with buyers and sellers, entertainers and preachers, men, women and children. There were distinct areas of the fair for selling different goods. Some of these names still appear as street names today, such as Garlic Row, Oyster Row and Mercers Row.

The fair, originally set up to care for lepers, continued for many centuries after the disease had disappeared. It finally closed in 1933.

Medieval fairs

Nowadays we think of fairs as fun. In medieval times fairs *were* fun, but were also meant for serious trade. People travelled from far and wide to stock up on everyday items, as well as to hunt down rare luxuries from further afield. Fairs often took place at the gates of a monastery, convent or hospital. This was so that the monks and nuns could charge fees and tolls to raise money to care for the poor.

There were three main fairs in Cambridge:

- *St Radegund's Convent Fair*, started under King Stephen. It was later called *Garlic Fair*.
- *Leper's Hospital Fair*, started under King John. It was later called *Stourbridge Fair*.
- *Barnwell Priory Fair*, started under Henry III. It later became known as *Midsummer Fair*.

Some visitors would stock up on their shopping for months ahead. These household records of Alice de Bryene of Acton Hall in Suffolk (1412–13) show us the types of items that the Steward bought at Stourbridge.

Stourbridge Fair attracted trade from all over Europe. Luxury goods were unloaded from sea-going ships onto smaller boats at the seaport of King's Lynn, ready for the final leg of the journey up the rivers Ouse and Cam.

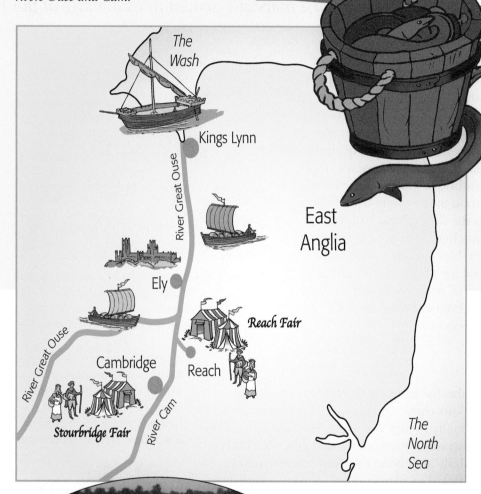

100 oysters 2d	Onions 5d
12 plaice 8d	Beef & Pork 4s 2d
Turbot 18d	Veal 20d
7 eels 16d	Eggs 15d
100 welkes 3d	1 Young Pig 6d
Bread for Merchant's horse $\frac{1}{2}$d	Pepper 3s 3d
	Cinnamon 4s 6d
Garlic 2$\frac{1}{2}$d	Iron pan 3s 4d

The Wash

Kings Lynn

River Great Ouse

Ely

River Great Ouse

Cambridge

Stourbridge Fair

River Cam

Reach Fair

Reach

East Anglia

The North Sea

In Cambridge, only Midsummer Fair survives today. It still opens every year on 22 June on Midsummer Common, just as it did in medieval times, though the modern fair would be barely recognisable to medieval fair-goers.

The power of the Church

In medieval times, the Church was rich, powerful and central to people's lives. Walking through the heart of Cambridge, there were at least ten churches in the short distance of a mile. This reflected the vital part the Church and its parishes played in the life of the town.

From the early 13th century, the Church's presence in Cambridge became even stronger as many young men arrived to study as clerks (priests) at the new university. The first friars also arrived in Cambridge at this time.

A great age of church-building

Most of the wooden churches in Cambridge were rebuilt in stone from the 12th century onwards. This shows that the town was becoming richer. Nearly all the beautiful churches we see in Cambridge today are medieval, although they were usually built on the sites of much older churches. Besides being used for worship, churches were regularly used for public events, church courts' sessions, meetings of gilds, and even as hospitals and schools.

Holy Trinity Church had to be completely rebuilt in stone in 1174 after the original church, built of wood, was burnt to ashes in one of many devastating fires that swept through Cambridge.

The religious gilds and Corpus Christi

Cambridge had over thirty gilds – social and religious clubs which supported its members, especially in times of need. The Gild of Corpus Christi was a particularly rich gild which met regularly at St Bene't's Church. Every year it celebrated its patron saint's feast day with a spectacular procession through the town.

In 1352 the gild was unique in setting up a new college in the University. Corpus Christi College was also the *only* college in Cambridge started by local citizens. It was set up at a time of desperate need to train new clergymen for the town. Priests were in very short supply after a catastrophic outbreak of the Black Death in 1349, which killed about one third of the local population in just nine months. The horror of the Black Death was to hang over the town for the next 300 years.

A rare 13th-century drinking horn, used by members of the Gild of Corpus Christi. It has belonged to Corpus Christi College for over 650 years and is still used on special occasions.

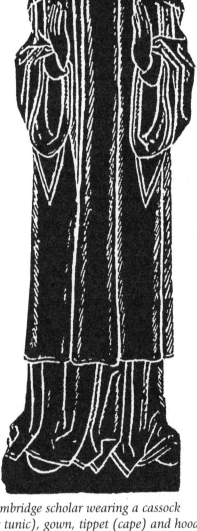

A Cambridge scholar wearing a cassock (long tunic), gown, tippet (cape) and hood. This brass memorial is in St John's College. In medieval times, the narrow streets of Cambridge would have been bustling with churchmen and women in religious dress: parish priests in their cassocks; monks in black capes; nuns in their wimples; friars in sackcloth habits; and scholars and clerks donning their dark academic gowns.

Monks and nuns

Monks and nuns played a key part in town life, even though most lived outside the town itself. They provided many services, including looking after the sick, giving alms to the poor, and offering rooms to travellers.

The richest, largest and oldest monastery in Cambridge was Barnwell Priory. The extensive buildings – including a library, refectory, guest hall, infirmary, granary, stables, bakery, brewhouse, gatehouse, two chapels and a church – were home to fewer than 20 monks, and their servants. The monastery soon gained a reputation as a more comfortable stop-over for royal visitors than the castle. In 1388, for example, King Richard II and his entire court lodged there as guests. The Priory was also renowned as a place for study and learning.

The monastery at Barnwell was completely overshadowed by the great Benedictine monastery in Ely, 17 miles away. This was where the Bishop of Ely was based. The bishops of Ely played a very important part in encouraging the early University of Cambridge.

The only convent in Cambridge was St Radegund. The nuns there grew their own vegetables, fished from the nearby brook and wove wool from their own sheep. The convent flourished, so much so that the nuns had a large and splendid stone church built in the 13th century. The stone was brought up the River Cam by boat. This church now forms part of the present-day chapel at Jesus College. By 1496, the nunnery was in such a bad state that the Bishop of Ely, John Alcock, closed it down. He replaced it with The College of the Blessed Virgin Mary, St John the Evangelist, and the Glorious Virgin St Radegund, near Cambridge. Luckily he agreed for it to be called Jesus College for short!

The friars

The friars were drawn to Cambridge to study theology as well as to teach and to preach. This had a lasting effect on the University. As scores of friars arrived in the town demanding university teaching, this encouraged the University to grow. The first Franciscan friars (Greyfriars) arrived in England in 1224, and within weeks they set up a house in Cambridge. The Dominicans (Blackfriars) settled in the town in 1238. The Austin Friars built their friary on St Bene't's Street in the late 13th century. In contrast to the monks and nuns, friars lived right in the middle of the town so that they could get to university lectures easily and preach directly to townspeople in the streets.

This is one of the few remains of a once glorious monastery, Barnwell Priory.

The old Jewish quarter

From Norman times, Cambridge had a large, flourishing Jewish quarter near All Saints' Passage. But in the late 13th century, some Christians stirred up suspicion and hatred against the Jews, and persecuted them. In 1275, the King and citizens of Cambridge expelled all Jews from the town.

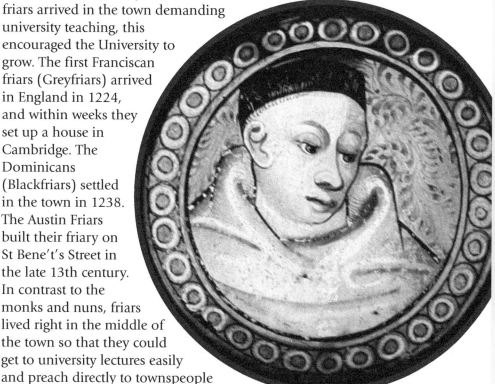

This friar is shown on a tiny and beautiful stained glass window. It was once in the chapel of the Carmelite Friary, and is now in Queens' College library.

A cross now marks the spot where the medieval church of 'All Saints Jewry' once stood. The church was demolished in 1865. This area was originally the Jewish quarter.

A new power: the University

In the early 13th century, a group of scholars fled from a dispute in Oxford and settled in Cambridge. This chance event marked the beginning of a new power in the land: the University of Cambridge.

The small band of scholars set up an advanced school with masters (teachers), scholars and a Chancellor as head. In 1291, Cambridge finally won royal approval as a university. In 1318, the Pope gave his approval too, and this made Cambridge an official university of European standing, along with those in Bologna, Padua and Paris.

The first scholars arrive in Cambridge

At the start of the 13th century Oxford was the only university in Britain. Then in 1209, a crisis flared up unexpectedly between the Town and University. Many Oxford scholars fled from the hostile townsmen and took refuge in nearby towns such as Reading. Some travelled further afield to Cambridge.

At first, there were no university or college buildings at all in Cambridge. Lectures were held wherever there was space, such as in St Bene't's Church.

The early student hostels

Nowadays, when we think of the early University, we often think of the colleges, but in fact for the first two centuries, most scholars lived in hostels. Later many of these hostels became colleges when they attracted endowments (money and land) from wealthy benefactors.

A hostel was rather like a boarding house. By 1280, there were over 30 hostels in Cambridge. There was usually a master in charge, but even so, discipline in the hostels was often lax. Many scholars, who were often only boys of 14 or 15, were involved in brawls with students from neighbouring hostels. To enforce greater discipline, some members of the University wanted to set up permanent colleges with stricter rules, or statutes.

Town and Gown

As the University grew, so did the squabbles between the *Town* and *Gown* (the University). The University thought that local citizens overcharged for rooms and food. They demanded cheaper rents for the scholars, as well as special rates for essentials such as bread, ale and candles. The citizens in turn thought the University had too many special privileges.

Tensions reached a peak in 1381 when the townspeople attacked the University. Even the mayor joined in as the angry town rebels rampaged into Great St Mary's Church and smashed open the University Chest.

The first colleges

In the late 13th century, the earliest colleges were set up as permanent places for scholars to live, study and, very importantly, pray.

In 1284, the Bishop of Ely, Hugh Balsham, decided that he needed somewhere to keep his unruly young scholars under control. First he lodged them in the Church of St Peter (now Little St Mary's) and then he moved them to some vacant houses next door. This was the origin of the first college, Peterhouse. After this, eight more colleges were founded in succession, before a lull of nearly 100 years.

Medieval master and scholars. Nearly all early scholars were priests. Notice their tonsures (shaved patches) and clerical robes.

College	Date started
• Peterhouse	1284
• King's Hall (later merged into Trinity College)	1317
• Michaelhouse (also merged into Trinity College)	1324
• University College (later refounded as Clare Hall)	1326
• Clare Hall (now Clare College)	1338
• Pembroke Hall (now Pembroke College)	1347
• Gonville Hall (later to become Gonville and Caius)	1348
• Trinity Hall	1349
• Corpus Christi	1352

Old Court at Corpus Christi. This is the oldest surviving courtyard in Cambridge, started in 1352. The early medieval courtyards were very modest and built of the local building material, clunch.

The lovely gardens and library at Trinity Hall. This college was founded by William Bateman, the Bishop of Norwich. In the mid-14th century, almost 700 parish priests in his diocese had died of the Black Death and Bateman urgently needed to train more priests.

Who gave the money for these colleges?

The colleges could not have been built without wealthy benefactors, or patrons, who gave large amounts of money for building projects, rather like modern-day sponsors. The early patrons were usually kings and queens, bishops or rich widows.

Most patrons had religious motives. They wanted to help the Church by setting up a place for priests to train. In return for their money, members of the college had to pray for the benefactor's soul after he or she had died, every day for eternity. This was considered very important in medieval times when people believed strongly in Heaven and Hell. Priests who had the full-time job of saying prayers for their souls were known as 'chantry priests'.

Some patrons liked to show off their acts of charity. College crests were therefore very popular. Patrons displayed their shields in the same way that a modern company likes to display its logo.

Lady Elizabeth de Clare, who founded Clare Hall (later Clare College). Wealthy widows were important patrons of the early colleges.

The foundress Lady de Clare was widowed three times. The arms of Clare College (left) are surrounded by gold teardrops on a black band, a poignant symbol of her grief.

Kings, queens and colleges

Nearly a century later, there was a new wave of college-building when some of the finest colleges in Cambridge were founded. The royal family started to take a great interest in Cambridge. King's College was begun by Henry VI in 1441, and Queens' College by his wife, Margaret of Anjou, in 1448. At that time, Oxford was the more important university of the two. But the King and Queen probably favoured Cambridge because the scholars at Cambridge were less heretical (critical of the Church).

King's College: a royal masterpiece

Henry VI was only 19 when he started King's College. He wanted it to be bigger and better than all the other colleges in Oxford and Cambridge. A typical college at that time had about 20 members, but Henry VI had plans for over 70 Fellows and scholars. He wanted King's College to educate priests, to preach against heresy and to glorify God. King's College Chapel was exceptionally tall and long for a private chapel. It had 10 altars and 10 chantry priests to say mass each day.

The college was planned as a double foundation. It was linked to another of Henry VI's great projects, Eton. This was a school for poor scholars who would go on to study at King's when they were 14. At both places, Henry was passionately concerned with the chapels and the teaching. Nearly 600 years later, the public school of Eton, as well as King's College, have survived spectacularly well as world-famous places of education.

King's and Queens': contrasting colleges

King's College was a truly large-scale project. Every building in the parish of St Zachary was knocked down to make space for the new college. It took three years to buy up the riverside stretch of land and clear it of houses, shops, the church and numerous lanes and wharves. Many townspeople lost their homes and livelihood in the royal demolition.

As King's took shape, the bustling Milne Street, or Mill Street (now Queens' Lane) declined into a shadow of its former self, whilst High Street (now King's Parade) grew in importance (compare maps on pages 21 and 33).

Queens' College was a much more modest project. It was the first college to be built to a simple courtyard design with chapel included (see pages 30–1). This basic blueprint was copied many times in the next two centuries.

Henry VI shown on the Founder's Charter of 1446, praying for his new college, King's. The Chapel was far from complete when he lost his throne in 1461. It was left to Henry VII to complete the building.

What is a college?

A college is first and foremost a community of teachers (Fellows) and students. A few of the Fellows live in the college, along with most of the students. At college the students eat, sleep, study, attend small group teaching sessions, called *supervisions*, and party!

Visitors to Cambridge sometimes ask, 'Where is the University?' It is impossible to point to any one particular place, as the University is all around them. In fact, the University is made up of 31 separate colleges spread all over the town.

Each college is independent, owns its own property and has its own income. Individual colleges also have their own distinct character and traditions.

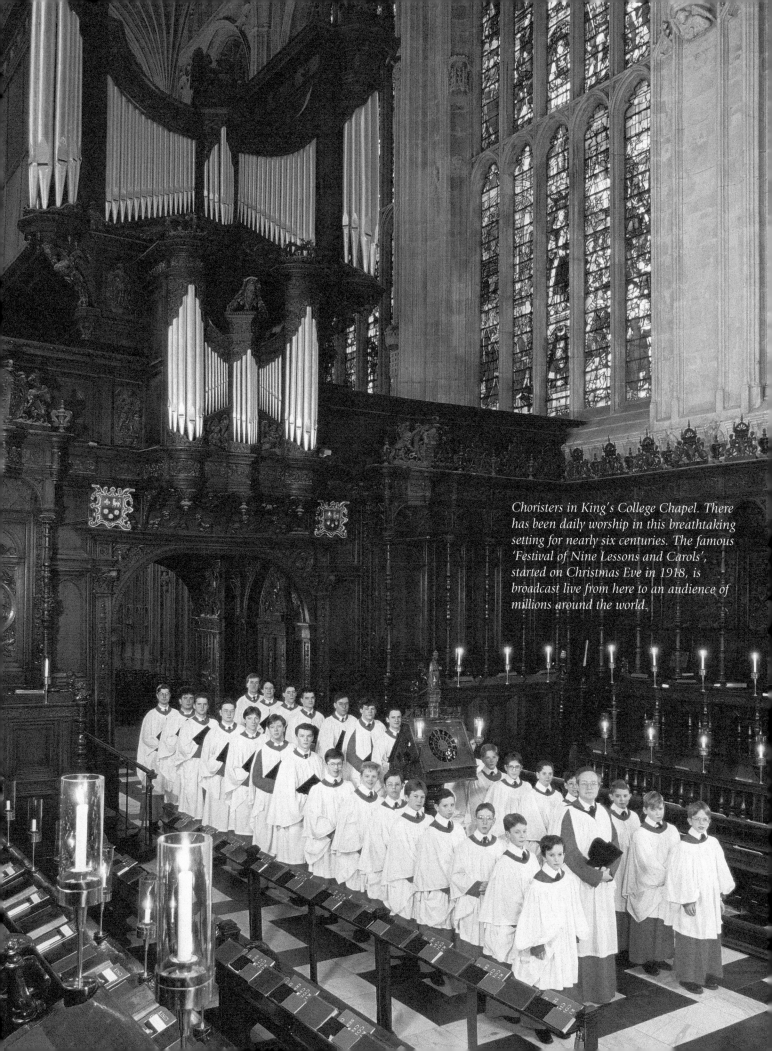

Choristers in King's College Chapel. There has been daily worship in this breathtaking setting for nearly six centuries. The famous 'Festival of Nine Lessons and Carols', started on Christmas Eve in 1918, is broadcast live from here to an audience of millions around the world.

Queens': a medieval college

Old Court at Queens' College is one of the few courts to have survived in its original medieval form. Entering this small, quiet courtyard from the busy streets outside is like stepping back in time.

Queens' was the first college to be purpose-built. Earlier colleges such as Peterhouse and Corpus had made use of existing churches (St Peter's and St Bene't's) and then built their living quarters nearby. Queens' was built to a simple design with hall, kitchens, library, chapel and chambers arranged around a square courtyard. This followed the pattern of a typical courtyard house of the time.

The royal patronesses

Queens' College is proud of its two founding queens, Margaret of Anjou and later Elizabeth Woodville. The college was originally the idea of a local priest at St Botolph's Church, Andrew Dokett. He had to work tirelessly to win the support of both queens for the new college. This was quite an achievement since they fought on opposite sides in the Wars of the Roses!

The old chapel
At the very heart of a college was its chapel. Margaret of Anjou (the first patron) insisted that mass should be held here twice a day.

The library
Libraries were usually on the first floor, as this one was, to avoid the damp and floods. They were also aligned from east to west to receive plenty of sunlight.

Queen Elizabeth Woodville, wife of Edward IV, was the second queen to give her support.

Queen Margaret of Anjou, wife of Henry VI, was only 18 when she gave money to set up Queens' College, and was the first queen to found a Cambridge college.

The gatehouse
This large gatehouse is like the entrance to a fortress. Gateways were mainly for show, but they were functional too. They kept scholars in, whilst keeping out thieves, trouble-makers and women!

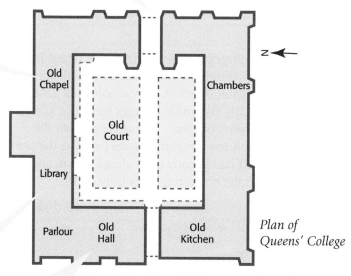

Plan of Queens' College

The Hall
Fellows and students used to dine together at 3 pm, their day having started early at dawn. The hall floor would be strewn with reeds, and heated by a simple brazier in the middle of the room. There was an opening in the roof to let smoke out. This is the original dining hall at Queens', used for over 500 years. The rich decoration on the walls and ceiling were added in the 19th century.

Life as a medieval scholar

In a typical college such as Queens', scholars used to share two or three to a room. They slept on trundle beds which were folded away during the day to make space for them to work. Getting up at daybreak (5 am in summer), the scholars first attended chapel services and then lectures.

Since candles were expensive, not much studying took place after dark. However, after a long day's work, many did find time to go to local alehouses, of which the small town had a very large number – probably about 80.

Scholars in medieval Cambridge must have been extremely hardy. Winters in Cambridge were notoriously cold and damp. Scholars lived in freezing rooms with no heating at all. (The only fire in the whole college was lit in the Hall.) The open staircases leading up to these rooms were often draughty. There was no glazing, and window openings had only simple wooden shutters to keep out the biting east wind.

Scholars spent much time copying up texts and discussing them. The master would teach from a precious handwritten copy.

Today, Queens' College looks very picturesque in the snow. But in the past, many scholars succumbed to fatal winter chills.

4 Tudor Cambridge

The gatehouse of St John's College, built in 1511. It has a glorious display of royal arms.

One of the greatest changes in English history was the Reformation, when the country changed from being Catholic to Protestant. It was a critical time for Cambridge. The Tudor kings and queens were forced to take more notice of the University because they desperately needed its help to resolve England's religious and political problems.

In the 16th century, many beautiful new colleges were built, including the magnificent royal college of Trinity. The academic quarter started to take over the whole riverside area of Cambridge. By the end of the Tudor period, the University was larger and richer, and now played a vital part in national events.

Royal eyes on Cambridge

In Tudor times, the University grew in prestige, particularly by helping King Henry VIII in his famous Divorce Case. But in return, the Tudor kings and queens now wanted to interfere more in university affairs. They tried to keep control of any Fellows who spoke out, especially in religious matters. Those with unpopular opinions could be sacked, or imprisoned in the Tower of London. In Tudor times, a total of five university Chancellors were executed: John Fisher (in 1535), Thomas Cromwell (in 1540), the Duke of Somerset (in 1551), the Duke of Northumberland (in 1553) and the Earl of Essex (in 1600). The University now had to tread very carefully indeed!

A century of college-building

Many new colleges were set up in Tudor times. In the early 16th century, three new colleges were founded, two of them by Lady Margaret Beaufort, a great patron of Cambridge. From the 1540s, five more colleges were also founded, mostly as a result of Henry VIII closing down the monasteries. A few religious houses (such as the priory of St Radegund) had already been closed down, and the King dissolved all the remaining ones from 1536.

New colleges	Date started
Jesus College (once the Priory of St Radegund)	1496
Christ's College	1505
St John's College (once the Hospital of St John)	1511
Monasteries closed down by Henry VIII	1536-40
Magdalene College (once Buckingham College)	1542
Trinity College	1546
Gonville and Caius	1558
Emmanuel College (once the Dominican Friary, Blackfriars)	1584
Sidney Sussex College (once the Franciscan Friary, Greyfriars)	1596

The President's Lodge at Queens' College. In the early 16th century, the simple lodge was extended into this beautiful timber-beamed building.

A map of Cambridge in 1574. This is the earliest original map of the town to survive. ➤

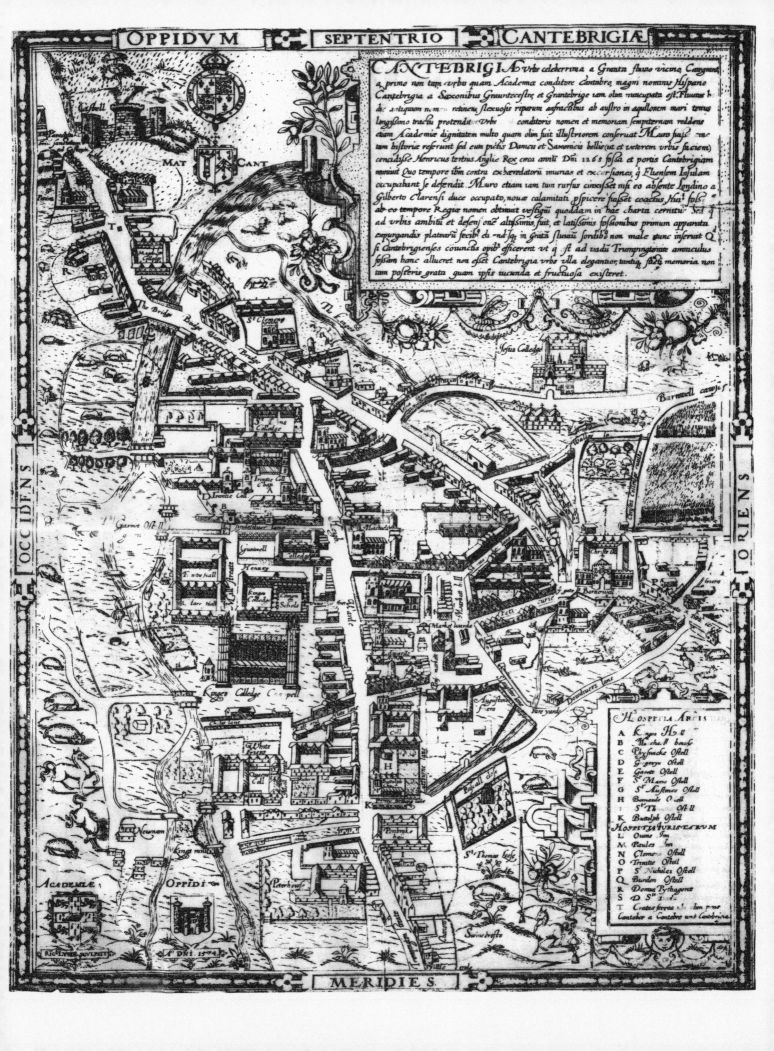

A new dynasty

Henry VII: the first Tudor king.

In 1485, Henry Tudor won the Battle of Bosworth, finally bringing the Wars of the Roses to an end. A new dynasty had begun. King's College Chapel, which had been left half-finished during the wars, gave Henry VII the perfect chance to show that it was the Tudors who were now in power.

Henry VII took a keen interest in Cambridge, as did his mother, Lady Margaret Beaufort, and her royal chaplain, John Fisher. They were both very pious and wanted to encourage learning. They also realised that more than ever, highly educated priests were needed to argue against the dangerous, heretical ideas which were spreading fast in Europe.

Cambridge's greatest patron

Lady Margaret Beaufort left her mark on Cambridge by founding two of the finest colleges in the University: Christ's College and St John's. She also set up the Lady Margaret Professorship of Divinity. This was the first Chair in Cambridge.

Like many early patrons, Lady Margaret was a very wealthy widow. A child bride at 7, she had married for the second time in 1456 to Edmund Tudor when she was just 12 years old. She gave birth to her only child, Henry – the future king – at 13. She was devastated when her son Henry VII died in 1509 and distracted herself from her grief by undertaking these large projects in Cambridge.

The Beaufort coat of arms is proudly emblazoned over the Master's Lodge at Christ's (above). The arms show two mythological beasts, called yales, holding the royal crest and the crown. The portcullis and red rose represent the Tudor family. The marguerite daisies are a pun on Margaret's name.

Lady Margaret Beaufort. As an old lady, she lived in the Master's Lodge at Christ's College.

Improving the University

During his thirty years as Chancellor of the University, John Fisher transformed Cambridge. The University gained new colleges, new professorships, new ideas and a new vitality. One of Fisher's greatest skills was to persuade rich and influential people such as Lady Margaret Beaufort to fund new projects. Fisher also encouraged his Dutch friend and brilliant scholar, Desiderius Erasmus, to stay in Cambridge. Erasmus lived here between 1510 and 1514, where he taught Ancient Greek for the first time at the University. This helped to open up the University to new Renaissance (humanist) ideas from the continent.

John Fisher was an outstanding Cambridge scholar in his own right. He was ordained a priest at the unusually young age of 22. Later he became the first Lady Margaret Professor of Divinity.

Erasmus: one of the most famous scholars in 16th-century Europe, who lived and taught in Cambridge.

Erasmus stayed at Queens' College where he lived in some rooms in Cloister Court, overlooking Silver Street. However, Erasmus did not like Cambridge much. He complained bitterly in a letter to a friend:

> I cannot go out of doors because of the plague ... I am beset with thieves, and the wine is no better than vinegar ... I do not like this place at all.

The Dragon is a symbol for Wales. It reminded people that the Tudor family originally came from the Principality of Wales.

The rose is a symbol for the Tudor family.

King's College Chapel. The fan-vaulting rises 24 metres high, giving a tremendous feeling of height, grandeur and grace.

King's College Chapel: Tudor glory

When Henry VII came to the throne, King's College was little more than a building site. The King employed a new architect to complete the work on the chapel. It had been built in fits and starts over a period of 70 years, interrupted by wars and shortages of money. Not surprisingly, over the years, the vision of the chapel had changed too. Henry VI had been inspired by piety. He decorated the chapel with beautiful carved angels. Henry VII, on the other hand, saw the chapel as a chance to display his power. He had it richly decorated with Tudor emblems – crowns, roses, greyhounds, dragons and portcullises.

A splendid new university church

Great St Mary's Church is one of the town's oldest churches, dating back to at least 1205. The University used it, from its earliest days, for meetings, lectures and degree ceremonies. Great St Mary's soon became the University Church, used by both Town and Gown. In the early 16th century, John Fisher had the church rebuilt to a more lavish design – the one we see today. Many people across the land gave generously, including Henry VII, who donated 100 oak trees from a nearby estate for the beautiful beamed roof.

Great St Mary's Church showed the growing power of the University. Even so, it was completely overshadowed by the chapel at King's, which was taking shape just across the street!

Henry VIII and royal Cambridge

Henry VIII: a strong and ruthless King. During his reign, Cambridge became very involved in the King's stormy affairs.

In 1529, Henry VIII set in motion a whole series of changes which dramatically reformed the English Church. When his first wife, Catherine of Aragon, failed to produce a son as heir to the throne, Henry asked for permission to divorce her. The Pope refused so the King cut off all links with Rome. England began to change from a Catholic to a Protestant country.

Between 1536 and 1540, the King closed down all the monasteries in the land, seizing their estates and riches. Would the Cambridge colleges also face the axe? Incredibly, the University not only survived, but grew stronger than ever. When Henry VIII founded Trinity College, the largest and most splendid college in Cambridge, this showed that royal support was guaranteed.

Luther and the first Protestants

Even before Henry's Divorce Crisis, religious trouble was brewing. In 1517, a German monk called Martin Luther attacked the Church and its bad practices. His supporters (Protestants) wanted to break right away from the Pope and set up a simpler Church.

Luther's ideas spread like wildfire and soon reached England. They were considered very dangerous indeed. Henry VIII and the bishops banned all copies of Luther's books. In Cambridge, his works were thrown onto a large bonfire outside the doors of Great St Mary's Church in 1520. Despite this swift action, the University was fast becoming a hotbed of Protestant ideas.

'Little Germany' and the first Protestant martyrs

During the 1520s, a small group of reformers (or Protestants) began meeting in secret at the White Horse Tavern in Cambridge. The group was nicknamed 'Little Germany' because its members discussed Luther's radical ideas – which originally came from Germany. The inn was situated down a dingy side street, close to where St Catharine's now stands. Members of Little Germany played a crucial part in turning England into a Protestant country, but they all took a very great risk. If caught, they could be tried for heresy and burned to death.

The first Protestant martyr from this group was Thomas Bilney. He was burned at the stake in Norwich in 1531. Other members included Robert Barnes, a friar-preacher who was burned to death in 1540 and Hugh Latimer, a Fellow of Clare College, who was put to death in Mary's reign.

Spreading the word

Speaking from the pulpit was a very powerful way to spread ideas in the 16th century. Protestants such as Barnes and Latimer often preached from St Edward's Church and nearby Great St Mary's. The Bishop of Ely used to arrive at their sermons unannounced, but failed to catch them in the act of preaching heresy.

Protestant ideas spread even more rapidly because printing had recently been invented in Germany. Cambridge was at the forefront of the printing revolution in England.

Latimer's pulpit in St Edward's Church.

In 1534, Henry VIII gave Cambridge University Press the right to print books. Since 1584, it has published books without a break, for over 400 years. This makes it the oldest printing and publishing house in the world.

The royal divorce

In 1529, Henry desperately wanted to get a divorce so he could marry Anne Boleyn and have a male heir. But he needed help from legal experts to win his case against the Pope. Henry turned to academics at Cambridge for help, knowing that some were secretly Protestants. He was helped in particular by a brilliant Cambridge scholar, Thomas Cranmer.

In 1535, Henry and his chief minister, Thomas Cromwell, made Henry VIII the Supreme Head of the Church. Everyone in the universities of Oxford and Cambridge had to swear an oath of loyalty to the King. Whilst Protestants swore the oath willingly, some Fellows were very unhappy to do so. One man was brave enough to stand up for his beliefs: John Fisher. He was beheaded in 1535 for preaching against the King.

Thomas Cranmer: a great reformer

Thomas Cranmer: a Cambridge scholar who became one of the most important people in the English Church.

When the Catholic queen, Mary, came to the throne, Cranmer was burnt at the stake for heresy in 1556, along with bishops Latimer and Ridley.

Thomas Cranmer: a great reformer

Cranmer was England's first Protestant archbishop and played a major part in shaping the Church of England that we know today. His life – mostly spent in Cambridge – took many twists and turns.

He was an orphan of just 14 when he came to Jesus College in 1503. He fell in love with Joan, the niece of the landlady at the Dolphin's Inn on Jesus Lane, and married her. But since college members were not allowed to marry, he was thrown out of Jesus. His wife died in childbirth a year later, so Cranmer was allowed back into college. Cranmer now led a quiet and scholarly life for the next 20 years.

However, in 1529 he was swept onto the national stage to deal with the 'King's Great Matter'. He had a chance meeting with two royal advisers who were very impressed with his arguments in favour of the Divorce. In 1533, Henry promoted Cranmer from college Fellow to the highest church position in the land – Archbishop of Canterbury.

In 1532, Cranmer had secretly (and illegally) re-married, this time to a Lutheran called Margaret. When he became Archbishop, he quickly had to send her into hiding. A popular story goes that his wife was kept hidden in a wooden chest!

As Archbishop, Cranmer ended the King's marriage to Catherine of Aragon in 1533, to Anne Boleyn in 1536 and to Anne of Cleves in 1540. Cranmer was also the main author of the *English Book of Common Prayer*. It was a triumph of scholarship for the translators (12 of the 13 were from Cambridge).

The Tudor gatehouse at Jesus College. When Cranmer joined the college, it had just been founded (in 1496). The new college provided for a Master, five Fellows, four youths, four boys, a schoolmaster and five servants.

The axe falls on the monasteries

Between 1536 and 1540, Henry VIII closed down all the monasteries and friaries in England. Hundreds of monks, friars and nuns were simply turned out onto the streets. In many parts of the country, the buildings and lands were given or sold to rich landowners who had backed the King. In Cambridge, it was the University that gained most. Trinity College, for example, was built using money and lands from 24 monasteries.

After Cambridge's monasteries and friaries were shut down, a number were later turned into new colleges. Barnwell Priory slowly fell to ruins. It was considered too far out of town to be turned into a college.

Colleges in danger

Despite gaining from the closure of the monasteries, the colleges themselves were in a very perilous position. In 1545, a new law was passed to shut down all the colleges and big chantries. Their wealth would go to the King. First though, Henry VIII needed to find out how much land and wealth Cambridge had. By a stroke of good luck, Henry decided to use three local Cambridge men, known as 'Visitors', to investigate. One of them was Matthew Parker.

Naturally, the Visitors – who were University men themselves – were keen to make out that the colleges were very poor. They cleverly persuaded the King that rather than shutting down colleges, he should start one of his own. It could be a magnificent college, packed with scholars who would be loyal to him, and at no cost at all! He could take over two existing colleges, King's Hall and Michaelhouse, seize Physwick Hostel, and make a new college dedicated to the Trinity. It proved an irresistible offer, and so Trinity College began.

Buckingham College, a hostel for Benedictine monks was re-founded as Magdalene College in 1542.

The Dominican Friary was re-founded as Emmanuel College in 1584.

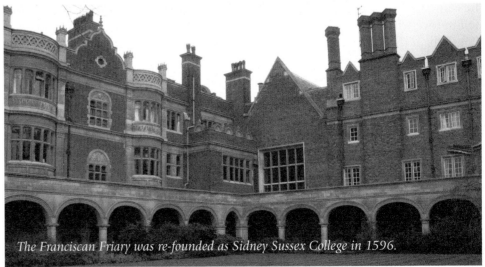

The Franciscan Friary was re-founded as Sidney Sussex College in 1596.

Trinity College

Trinity College is a fabulous college on a huge scale. The vast enclosed courtyard, called Great Court, is one of the largest in Europe.

The royal connection with Trinity remains strong to this day. Trinity is the only college where the Master is appointed by the Crown, and not chosen by the Fellows. It was also the college chosen for the Prince of Wales, Prince Charles, when he was a student at Cambridge in 1967.

Henry VIII − founder of the college − stands proudly over the Great Gate of Trinity. He is holding an orb in one hand and what looks like a sceptre in the other. However the sceptre is actually a wooden chair leg! The sceptre was removed as a practical joke over 50 years ago and the chair leg has remained there ever since.

Great Court at Trinity. Despite its harmonious appearance, the court is an irregular shape made up of a hotchpotch of styles. The oldest part is King Edward's Tower (left) built in the early 15th century. The Great Gate (right) was originally built as the gatehouse to King's Hall. The chapel (centre) was begun by Mary Tudor in 1554, in memory of her father, Henry.

'Chariots of Fire'

There is a tradition that undergraduates try to sprint round the perimeter of Great Court at Trinity whilst the college clock is striking midnight. The clock takes 45 seconds to strike and the distance is 370 metres, so it is by no means easy. In 1988, a race was set up between two Olympic runners, Sebastian Coe and Steve Cram. They only just achieved the feat which Lord Burghley, the Olympic athlete, had first managed in 1927. His achievements were portrayed in the Oscar-winning film *Chariots of Fire*, in 1981.

Great Court was re-designed by the Master, Thomas Nevile, in 1593. He added an Elizabethan dining hall as well as this lovely fountain.

Catholics and Protestants

In the following fifty years, the official religion in England changed three times, as each of Henry VIII's children came to the throne – Edward VI, Mary I and then Elizabeth I. With each new ruler, the Cambridge colleges had to change direction abruptly too. This was a very dangerous time for scholars of strong beliefs, as a number discovered to their terrible cost.

Edward VI. England became Protestant for the first time when the 10-year-old prince became King in 1547.

Edward VI and the Protestant changes

When Edward VI came to the throne, England gradually became Protestant. Cambridge played a crucial part in the changes that followed.

In 1549 the University invited the famous and fiery Protestant preacher from Germany, Martin Bucer, to become the Regius Professor of Divinity. This was an influential job. Bucer quickly made an impression as an exceptional preacher and scholar. At his funeral two years later, his coffin was followed to Great St Mary's Church by a huge procession of 3,000 people from Town and Gown.

Protestant changes were now happening fast. In Cambridge, churches and chapels were stripped of their splendid altars, crucifixes, rood screens and silver plate. The Protestants wanted simply furnished places of worship that did not distract from the Word of God. At Great St Mary's Church, the high altar and five side altars were pulled down in 1550 and replaced with simple communion tables. The frescoes (showing scenes from the Bible) were painted-over with whitewash. Protestants pasted writings from Scripture on the walls instead.

Lady Jane Grey: the nine-day Queen

In 1553, there was a botched attempt to put Lady Jane Grey on the throne. The 16 year-old King had unexpectedly died and Cambridge suddenly found itself right at the centre of national events. The Duke of Northumberland led a plot to make Lady Jane, a Protestant claimant, the new Queen instead of Princess Mary, the rightful heir. He sent a note to Mary from her brother Edward (who was already dead!), summoning her to London. But instead, she fled to Sawston Hall near Cambridge, for safety. Four thousand troops on foot and on horseback clattered through the narrow cobbled streets of Cambridge as Northumberland tried to seize control.

But the plot failed and there were riots in the town as Northumberland's troops deserted him. He was forced to declare Mary as rightful Queen on Market Hill.

The Duke was arrested in King's College and sent to the Tower. He was put to death on the scaffold. Lady Jane Grey was Queen for just nine days: she too was later executed.

A gruesome scene on the Market Square in 1556: Bucer's remains being publicly burned. Queen Mary was determined to make an example of the Protestant preacher.

Mary I and the English martyrs

Cambridge was now so important that, from the outset, the new Catholic Queen knew she had to deal with the Protestants there. All the college heads except for three were either sacked or forced to resign, and replaced by Catholics. Queen Mary also made all scholars swear an oath of loyalty. Many Protestant Fellows refused and fled abroad, fearing for their lives.

Protestants were now strictly forbidden to worship. Nearly 300 Protestants, including over 30 from Cambridge, were burned at the stake as heretics. College chapels were re-decorated in their earlier Catholic style. Many chaplains simply put back their original Catholic furnishings which they had cunningly hidden away during Edward's reign!

In 1556, one particular event shook the country to the very core. Three much respected churchmen were burned at the stake for their Protestant beliefs: Archbishop Cranmer, Bishop Latimer and Bishop Ridley. They died in Oxford, but they had all been Fellows at Cambridge.

Mary I. She came to the throne in 1553, and brought back the Catholic religion.

Only one Protestant was burned to death in Cambridge, here on Jesus Green. A large crowd gathered to watch as John Hullier, once a chaplain at King's College, was tied to the stake. It was a blustery day and the fire was badly set. One of his friends gave him bags of gunpowder to hang round his neck to speed up his death. Many local people were sickened by the event.

Papists and priestholes

Catholics – or Papists – caught practising their religion were considered heretics and traitors. Their punishment could be death. Catholics set up hiding places in country houses where they could conceal their priests in times of danger. When the houses were searched, priests sometimes had to hide in the tiny 'priestholes' for days at a time.

The main Catholic family in Cambridgeshire was the Huddlestons of Sawston. Sir John Huddleston had been knighted after helping Queen Mary in 1553. In Elizabeth's reign, Sir Edmund Huddleston (son of Sir John) secretly carried on being a Catholic, at tremendous personal risk.

Priest's hiding hole at Sawston Hall, built in 1592. Through the trapdoor there was just room to crouch. There are three priest holes altogether at Sawston Hall. They were so well disguised that two of them remained undiscovered until 1959.

Queen Elizabeth I and the Protestant peace

In 1558, Mary died and the Protestant exiles flooded back to England, full of hope. The new queen, Elizabeth I, at once made important changes in Cambridge. Eleven college heads who were Catholics were replaced by Protestants.

Elizabeth tried to make the Church of England a broad church, acceptable to people with a wide range of religious views. She appointed Matthew Parker, a moderate Protestant, as her new Archbishop of Canterbury. He proved an excellent choice. He introduced the Thirty-Nine Articles in 1559, and these still underpin the teaching of the Church of England today. Her long reign from 1558 to 1603 meant that the Protestant religion was well established by the time she died.

Elizabethan Cambridge

During Elizabeth I's reign, the number of students at Cambridge soared to record levels, and for the first time, many were from gentlemanly backgrounds. This was to have a great effect on the University.

At the same time, Queen Elizabeth took a great personal interest in Cambridge, especially after a very successful royal visit. As a result, the University became closer to royal power than it ever had been, or ever would be again.

Queen Elizabeth loved the scholarly environment at Cambridge and impressed the Fellows with her remarkable intellect.

A royal guest at Cambridge

In 1564, Queen Elizabeth visited Cambridge and stayed at King's. All 14 colleges had to accommodate (for free) the great retinue of courtiers and servants who accompanied her. The town stocked up with huge quantities of beer, ale and wine. Elizabeth arrived on horseback and crowds flocked to see the royal procession arriving along Silver Street. During her five-day visit, the Queen attended – and enormously enjoyed – hours of church sermons, disputations in Latin and Greek, as well as numerous plays and feasts.

The town was drunk dry. The University basked in the glory and Cambridge graduates greatly benefited from the visit. The Queen now surrounded herself with Cambridge-educated courtiers. She also chose Cambridge men (rather than Oxford ones) to hold most of the high positions of the land, following the example of her chief adviser, William Cecil (Lord Burghley).

A flood of gentlemen

In medieval times, most scholars were clerks, training to be priests. The majority came from poor backgrounds: we know this from letters they wrote, begging for money. In Elizabeth's reign, this changed dramatically as rich nobles and gentlemen began to send their sons to Cambridge. Many had grown richer after buying up monastery lands in Henry VIII's reign. They now wanted to send their sons to university to reflect their growing wealth and social status. Many 16th-century scholars went on to train as lawyers, or travelled abroad for leisure. The arrival of so many gentlemen-scholars was to have a great impact on college-building in Cambridge (see pages 44–5 and 48–9).

There were four categories of scholars at Cambridge, depending on wealth and status:

- *Noblemen* paid high fees and had many privileges (such as sitting at the high table with the Fellows).
- *Fellow-commoners* were gentlemen but were not as rich as the noblemen. They also paid college fees for board and lodging.
- *Pensioners* were charged more moderate fees for basic board and lodging.
- *Sizars* were the poorest scholars. They paid their way by *sizing* (doing menial tasks such as sweeping and waiting on the Fellows at high table).

There was no mistaking who was who, as the scholars wore different caps and gowns to mark them out. This social ranking lasted until the early 19th century.

A gentleman-scholar

John Harvard, who founded the first university in the United States, based on his old Cambridge college. This is part of a stained glass window in the chapel at Emmanuel.

Puritan Cambridge

In the late 16th century, Cambridge became a hotbed of Puritan ideas. Puritans were extreme Protestants who wanted the Church of England to become 'purer' and simpler. They felt very encouraged when two new Cambridge colleges – Emmanuel and Sidney Sussex – were set up. These were, in effect, training grounds for Puritan preachers.

But despite this success, the Puritans became increasingly disenchanted with the Queen. In the 1630s, many graduates from Emmanuel sailed to North America to set up new colonies where they could worship more freely. One of these Puritans, John Harvard, started a new college in Cambridge, Massachusetts. This college, Harvard, is now a world-famous university.

Scholars and their pastimes

There was a downside to this influx of rich students. Some were accused of being lazy, more interested in gambling with dice and keeping greyhounds, than in their studies. They wore fancy ruffs, velvet pantaloons and brightly coloured stockings. This was in stark contrast to the sober clothing of the medieval clerks just a hundred years before.

The colleges were constantly issuing bans. St John's forbade ferrets, hawks and singing-birds. Gonville and Caius banned archery, axe-hurling and bear-baiting. They also tried – unsuccessfully – to prevent students from playing football. The game of football was often a rowdy free-for-all in Tudor times. There was a particularly violent game in 1579, when the scholars played against the townsmen at the nearby village of Chesterton. It seems that the townsmen got the better of the gownsmen for they:

> did bring out their staves [sticks] wherewith they did so beat the scholars that diverse had their heads broken.

A golden age of theatre and poetry

Theatre, on the other hand, was very much encouraged at Cambridge. At Queens' College, performing or attending college plays was even made compulsory. Corpus Christi, in particular, attracted some shining talent in the late 16th century, including Christopher Marlowe.

Poetry also flourished spectacularly in Elizabethan Cambridge. The widely acclaimed poet, Edmund Spenser, was a sizar at Pembroke, and later wrote his most famous poem, *The Faerie Queene*, inspired by Elizabeth I.

Christopher Marlowe: dramatist and poet

Marlowe came to Corpus in 1581 where he spent six colourful years. He was only just granted his masters degree, because the University suspected he was secretly a Catholic. He left for London where he wrote famous plays such as *Tamburlaine* and *Dr Faustus*. His bold and passionate characters mirrored his own dramatic life and death. In 1593, aged just 29, he was stabbed in the eye with a dagger in a Deptford tavern brawl and died from the wound.

Marlowe's brilliant work paved the way for Shakespeare's outstanding achievements.

Emmanuel College was founded by the Puritan, Sir Walter Mildmay, who was Chancellor of the Exchequer to the Queen. The original friary church became the dining hall, which was freshly white-washed in Puritan style.

5 The 17th and 18th centuries

The mid-17th century was a time of tremendous upheaval in England. In 1642, Civil War broke out between the King and Parliament. Cambridge found itself once again in the midst of dramatic change. The town became a military headquarters for the Parliamentarians. Oliver Cromwell, who led the Parliamentarian army and later ran the country as Lord Protector, was the MP for Cambridge.

When Cromwell died, the monarchy was restored. Charles II became King in 1660, and the Cambridge colleges celebrated. A welcome period of peace and prosperity followed. From the 1660s, there was a great age of science and architecture in Cambridge, inspired by the towering genius of two men: Sir Isaac Newton, a Trinity scholar, and Sir Christopher Wren.

Sir Christopher Wren designed elegant classical buildings that changed the face of English towns and cities – including Cambridge, Oxford and London.

Cambridge in the age of Newton and Wren. Both men were exceptional mathematicians, but each used their genius in different ways.

Fine new buildings and bridges

In the 17th and 18th centuries, Cambridge was transformed as many lovely courts, chapels, libraries and bridges sprung up in the university quarter. Most were designed in a classical style by architects such as Sir Christopher Wren and James Gibbs. Many of the buildings were added to existing colleges to provide grander accommodation for the growing number of gentlemen-scholars. From the early 17th century, a light-coloured stone called Ketton Stone was increasingly used (rather than the local material, clunch, or the distinctive red bricks of early Tudor times). This gave the new buildings a glorious, golden glow.

The crowded town: squalor and stench

Quayside, Magdalene Street and Bridge Street are a few of the surviving areas of Cambridge which give a feel of the 17th-century working town. The timber-framed houses appear picturesque to us today, but living conditions there must have been cramped and filthy. As the local population grew, town buildings like these were divided into an ever greater number of separate lodgings. Sanitation was extremely basic. Many townspeople dumped waste, rubbish and muck straight onto the streets, into the river or into the King's Ditch which skirted the town. Wild dogs ran loose in the streets. Trinity College even had to employ a man to keep scavenging animals out of the chapel!

Sir Isaac Newton, Professor in mathematics at Cambridge, developed brilliant new theories about how the world worked.

A classical masterpiece: the Wren Library at Trinity College, designed by Christopher Wren.

Contrasting Cambridge

Visitors were quick to draw the contrasts between the splendid colleges and the impoverished town. A lady called Celia Fiennes, who travelled around England side-saddle, was delighted by the river landscapes of Cambridge:

> 1697
> St John's College Garden is very pleasant for the fine walks, both close shady walks and open rows of trees and quickset hedges ... Claire Hall [now Clare College] is very little but most exactly neat; in all parts they have walks with rows of trees and bridges over the river and fine painted gates into the fields.

In contrast, the famous diarist, John Evelyn, described Cambridge like this:

> 1654
> ... the whole town is a low dirty unpleasant place, the streets ill-paved, the air thick and infected by the fens ...

But like many scholars, the poet Thomas Gray was sad to leave Cambridge when he had finished his studies. He wrote in a letter:

> 1738
> I don't know how it is, I have a sort of reluctance to leave this place ... 'tis true Cambridge is very ugly, she is very dirty, & very dull; but I'm like a Cabbage, where I'm stuck, I love to grow.

He later returned to Cambridge and made it his home.

Little St Mary's churchyard. The 18th-century poet, Thomas Gray, studied at Peterhouse which overlooks this intimate churchyard. Perhaps it provided early inspiration for his famous poem, 'Elegy written in a Country Churchyard'.

Magdalene Street today. In the 17th century many of these houses would have been inns and merchant homes. Behind them, dingy narrow yards and alleyways led to warehouses and wharves which backed onto the river.

Civil War

In 1642, a long-standing quarrel between King Charles I and Parliament erupted into full-scale war. The King believed he could rule without advice from Parliament and was backed by the Royalists. The Parliamentarians, who were mostly Puritans, wanted Parliament to have more power. During the bloody war, many thousands of men died.

Many people tried to keep out of the conflict. But the citizens of Cambridge had little choice as Cambridge was in a strongly Puritan area. Oliver Cromwell was the town's MP and soon became a Puritan army leader too. He and his troops seized control of Cambridge and occupied the castle for the first time in centuries.

Divided England in 1642. Cambridge held an important strategic position in the eastern region.

Puritan town, Royalist gown

Cambridge is often described as Puritan, in contrast to Royalist Oxford (which was the King's headquarters). But when war was declared, Cambridge was in fact dangerously split. Most townspeople supported Parliament, whereas the University mainly backed the King.

Most of the Cambridge colleges clearly showed their royalist feelings when Charles I returned from Scotland in 1641. They celebrated by lighting huge bonfires in the streets of Cambridge. The citizens of Cambridge, on the other hand, were generally pro-Cromwell. They had chosen Cromwell as their Member of Parliament in 1640. He had once been a student at the Puritan college of Sidney Sussex and was a local gentleman-farmer who owned land in Huntingdon and Ely.

In 1642, there was a very tense atmosphere in the streets of Cambridge as the townspeople took up arms, supplied by Cromwell. Some even used the college coats of arms for firing practice!

Charles I had a lot of support from the University. Many colleges gave their valuable silver plate to his cause.

Cromwell had strong local roots. He lived in this house in Ely from 1636 to 1647.

Oliver Cromwell had great support from the Town. Before 1642, Cromwell had never been a soldier. But within a few years he proved himself as a brilliant general.

This is a black felt hat worn by Cromwell in Parliament. It shows his simple Puritan style.

Cambridge becomes a Puritan stronghold

Cambridge soon became the headquarters for the Eastern Counties Association, a Puritan association of five rebel counties. In 1642, Cromwell's troops rebuilt Cambridge castle. They dismantled the wooden bridges spanning the River Cam (such as the bridges at St John's and Trinity), to make the town more secure, and fortified the town with ditches. Puritan soldiers filled the streets. There were many horror stories of Puritans plundering the town. But Cambridge was in a sense lucky: it was so well defended that the Royalists never besieged it, sparing the town a lot of death and destruction.

Puritan purges

In a Puritan stronghold, it was very risky to support the King. Yet some of the college heads were openly Royalist, including the Masters at St John's, Jesus and Queens'. They were arrested and imprisoned in the Tower of London (but not actually put to death). By 1643, 11 Royalist heads of colleges had been forced to leave their positions.

In 1649, Charles I was executed and Cromwell became Lord Protector. All the Cambridge college heads, Fellows and students had to swear an oath to the new Commonwealth of England. Most did so, but three more college heads were dismissed for refusing.

The Puritans set out to destroy anything they considered 'superstitious', or Papist, such as raised altars, pictures and statues of saints and cherubs. The man chosen to demolish them in Cambridge was William Dowsing. Many religious works of art in college chapels and local churches were destroyed. Dowsing wrote in his journal:

> At Queens' College, December; 26 [1643]
> We beat down 110 superstitious pictures besides cherubims and engravings, where none of the Fellows would put on their hats in all the time they were in the chapel, and we digged up the steps for 3 hours and brake down 10, or 12 Apostles and Saints within the Hall.

Not much visible evidence of the Civil War remains in Cambridge today. The castle has long since disappeared. This picture shows how the castle gatehouse looked in the early 19th century.

Puritan soldiers occupying Trinity College during the War. The colleges were expected to provide food and lodgings for the soldiers.

Over 1,000 pictures were seized or destroyed in King's College Chapel on the same day. Miraculously, the beautiful stained glass survived.

What became of Oliver Cromwell?

Cromwell died in 1658 and was buried in Westminster Abbey. Yet strangely, his head came to be re-buried in the gardens of Sidney Sussex in Cambridge over 300 years later. How did this happen?

When Cromwell died he was given the full pomp of a State Funeral. However, two years later, Charles II was restored to the throne, and the Royalists were determined to get their revenge. Cromwell's body was dug up, dragged through the streets of London and hanged from the gallows. His head was then hacked off and stuck on a pole outside Westminster Hall where the gruesome sight remained until 1684.

From there, in a stormy gust of wind, Cromwell's head blew off the pole, landing at the feet of a sentinel on duty. The soldier tucked the head under his jacket, and later hid it up his chimney! He only told of its existence on his deathbed. For the next three centuries the head passed from collector to collector, finally reaching Cromwell's old college. Believed by experts to be the genuine remains, with spike hole still evident, his head was re-buried outside the chapel in 1960, where it has remained ever since.

Cromwell's embalmed head, now buried in Cambridge.

Classical Cambridge

In the 17th and 18th centuries there was a great period of building and landscaping in Cambridge. Many stunning college courts, chapels and libraries were built in the popular new classical style. Some of the finest buildings in Cambridge were designed by the famous architect, Sir Christopher Wren.

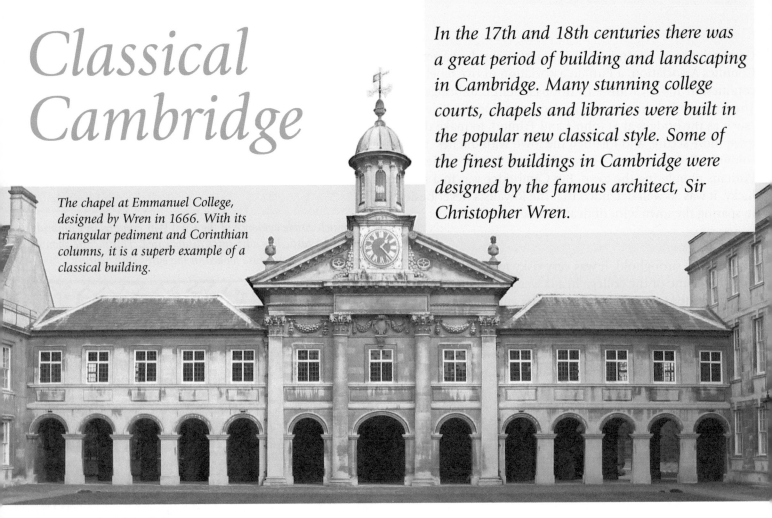

The chapel at Emmanuel College, designed by Wren in 1666. With its triangular pediment and Corinthian columns, it is a superb example of a classical building.

A new style of buildings

In the late 16th century, the traditional idea of a medieval college with its small, enclosed courtyard and castellated gatehouse, gave way to a new classical style. Architects began to borrow ideas taken from the buildings of ancient Greece and Rome. They built more open courts and included classical details such as arches, columns, pediments and statues.

In Cambridge, one of the first examples of this classical style was at Gonville and Caius. In 1557, a rich doctor, John Caius, transformed the existing Gonville Hall into a much larger college. He was inspired by the architecture he had seen whilst studying medicine at Padua University. He planned a three-sided Italian-style court that was open on one side. This was meant to encourage air to circulate more freely so that it should not become 'foul' – particularly important in a plague-ridden town such as Cambridge. The idea of the three-sided court was soon copied at many other colleges.

In the 17th century, the classical style flourished. Many fine buildings sprung up, including Nevile Court at Trinity, the Fellows' Building at Christ's College, and Old Court at Clare College. From the 1660s, Christopher Wren, the master of the classical style, designed the beautiful chapels at Pembroke and Emmanuel, and the Wren Library at Trinity College (see opposite and page 45).

An important reason for this boom in classical building was that there was a growing number of gentlemen-scholars coming to Cambridge. Colleges therefore had to provide more living quarters and larger chapels (to accommodate all the scholars for daily prayers).

When Samuel Pepys died in 1703, he left his book collection to his college, Magdalene. It is kept here in the Pepys Library at Magdalene. The priceless collection has 3,000 volumes, including his famous handwritten diary. In the 17th and 18th centuries many new and larger libraries were built as places to study and to store an ever increasing number of books.

Landscaping the Backs

Before the 17th century, the backs of the colleges were the equivalent of the tradesmen's entrance. Here, deliveries of wine, fuel and other bulky goods were made by barge. It was no accident that the west face of Wren's new library, which backed onto the river, was plainer in design, for it was not generally admired from the river as it is today.

However, from the late 17th century the Backs were gradually transformed. Landscaped gardens replaced garden plots, orchards and marshland. The Master of Trinity College, Richard Bentley, for example, had the land leading down to the river drained and made into lush meadows. It was later planted with weeping willows and avenues of lime trees.

Scenic bridges were built along the Cam. Many of the new stone bridges, such as Trinity Bridge, replaced those that Cromwell's soldiers had pulled down (see page 47).

Christopher Wren: Cambridge connections

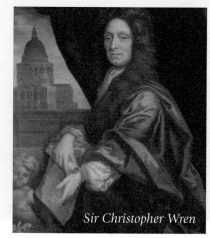

Sir Christopher Wren

Christopher Wren was from a strongly Royalist family. As a boy, he was a playmate of the future king, Charles II. His uncle, Matthew Wren, was a Fellow at Pembroke, later Master of Peterhouse and then Bishop of Ely, so was a well-known figure in Cambridge. When Civil War broke out, the unfortunate bishop was locked up in the Tower of London (for being a Royalist) for 18 years.

Christopher Wren, a brilliant scientist-mathematician, went to Oxford University. He became Professor of Astronomy there in 1661, and experimented with subjects ranging from sundials to submarines. He made his name as an architect, though, and his first foray into architecture was at Cambridge.

In 1663 his bishop-uncle (now released from the Tower) asked his nephew to design a chapel for Pembroke College. This miniature masterpiece was quickly followed by more commissions. The Master of Trinity, Isaac Barrow, a fellow mathematician, approached Christopher Wren for a new library. The result was the beautiful Wren Library.

The Wren Library. Nowadays, many people come to enjoy this view from the Backs.

An oddball bridge

Students sometimes challenge visitors to count the number of stone balls on Clare Bridge. At first glance, there are 14, but on closer inspection there are actually $13\frac{7}{8}$! No one knows why a segment of stone was cut away from the second ball on the right.

Clare College Bridge was built between 1638 and 1640. It is the oldest surviving bridge on the Cam.

A Romantic landscape

The avenues of trees alongside the gently flowing river became a favourite spot for young Romantic poets such as Wordsworth, Coleridge and, later, Byron to wander and contemplate. The Romantic poets liked to focus on nature and use ordinary words to express their personal feelings.

William Wordsworth came to St John's in 1787, arriving after a long journey from his home in the Lake District. He was full of excitement as he stepped down from his carriage. Here he describes his first impressions of Cambridge in a famous autobiographical poem:

> I was the Dreamer, they the Dream; I roamed
> Delighted through the motley spectacle;
> Gowns grave, or gaudy, doctors, students, streets,
> Courts, cloisters, flocks of churches, gateways, towers:
> Migration strange for a stripling of the hills
> A northern villager.
> Part of the *Prelude* by William Wordsworth

Science, medicine and witchcraft

In the 17th century, Cambridge became a centre for great advances in science, medicine and mathematics. The genius of one mathematician in particular shone out: that of Sir Isaac Newton.

The early years spent by Newton in Cambridge happened to coincide with a devastating outbreak of the plague. In 1665, the deadly illness swept through towns and villages in England, and the University even had to close down for a while. At a time when Newton was making some of the most brilliant scientific discoveries, the people of Cambridge were turning to prayers, folk cures and witchcraft in the face of a terrifying disease.

A GENERAL BILL

Of all those that have died in Cambridge of the Plague, other Diseases, from June the 5th to January the 1. 166

All the Colledges (God be praised) are and have continue without any Infection of the Plague.

	Bur.	Pla.	Infected & Recovered		Bur.	Pla.	Inf Rec
St Andrews Cambridge,	161	139	100	St Giles	027	015	
St Andrews Barnwell	063	053	083	St Maries Great,	048	032	
All-Saints	097	090	030	St Maries Less,	014	012	
St Bennetts	062	051	023	St Michael	019	013	
St Botolph	030	013	009	St Peters	012	003	
St Clements	021	012	006	St Sepulchres	024	017	
St Edwards	016	006	003	Trinity	153	138	

The total of Burials in the fourteen Parishes	
Whereof of the Plague	594
And at the Pesthouse	155
In all of the Plague.	749
Persons infected that are recovered	384
The total of Burials in both Visitations	1114
Whereof of the Plague	092

Francis Wilford *Vice-chancellour.*   John Herring

This Plague Bill sets out the number of deaths from the plague in Cambridge in just seven months from June 1665 to January 1666.

A new approach to science and medicine

Until the late 16th century, scholars drew on ancient Greek and Roman writings and the teachings of the Church to explain the world around them. This approach was challenged by scholars such as Sir Francis Bacon (who later became Lord Chancellor of England). Bacon carried out many scientific experiments – something we take for granted now but was considered very radical then.

A life-size marble statue of Francis Bacon in Trinity College. He died performing what was to be his final experiment in 1626. He got out of his carriage to stuff a dead chicken with snow to find out if the cold would preserve it. It did, but tragically Bacon caught a fatal chill.

In the early 17th century there were tremendous advances in medicine too. For the first time, doctors in England began to observe the human body itself, rather than studying the ancient medical writings. The physician John Caius, who had studied medicine at Padua (the leading university for medicine in Europe at that time), encouraged this new approach. Caius became a very rich and successful royal doctor. He gave much money to his old college, Gonville Hall, which had become poor and dilapidated, and re-founded it as Gonville and Caius College. It rapidly gained a strong reputation in medicine, which continues to this day.

Other famous physicians who studied at Caius include Stephen Perse, who founded a boys' school in Cambridge in 1618 (originally in Free School Lane), and William Harvey, probably England's first great medical scientist.

The plague rages

During the 17th century, there were frequent outbreaks of the plague in Cambridge. In the 1630s, strict new rules were introduced to stop the deadly disease from spreading. For example, there was a ban on people and goods entering or leaving the town during an outbreak, since it was believed that the disease could be carried on clothing.

In spite of these precautions, the plague struck the town with even greater vengeance in 1665. The University stood deserted as Fellows and scholars fled to nearby villages. Newton escaped to his home in Lincolnshire. When the plague was at its height, mass graves had to be built on Midsummer Common.

Newton's apple tree outside Trinity College. It is directly descended from a tree that grew at Newton's home, Woolsthorpe Manor in Lincolnshire.

Isaac Newton: a mathematical genius

In 1661, Isaac Newton came to Cambridge as a young man of 19. He was to become one of the greatest mathematicians ever. At the age of just 27 he was made Lucasian Professor of Mathematics. Newton lived and worked at Trinity for about 35 years, some of those years spent as a total recluse. His ideas have had a huge effect on how we understand the world. His most famous book, *Principia Mathematica*, published in 1687, took the country by storm. It overthrew religious beliefs of how the natural world was ordered.

One of Newton's most important discoveries was the law of gravity – the force that pulls objects towards the ground. The story goes that whilst reading a book under a tree, an apple happened to fall. Newton was immediately curious as to what makes things fall and came up with his ground-breaking ideas on gravity. He also explained how planets move around the sun, and moons move round planets.

Hobson's conduit (fountain) in Lensfield Road. It originally stood in the market place. The water supply started from a natural spring at Nine Wells, near Shelford. The water can still be seen today, flowing along the roadside in Trumpington Street.

A clean water supply for the town

The causes of the plague were little understood in the 17th century; it was seen as a punishment sent by God. However, a few forward-thinking doctors in the University, such as the Master of Peterhouse, Dr Perne, thought the filthy state of the river, drinking wells, and in particular the King's Ditch, were part of the problem. In 1610, a local businessman, Thomas Hobson (see page 53), built the first water supply for the town. Its main aim was to flush out the ditch with water. This did not work, but the town did receive fresh spring water for the next 250 years.

A carved wooden 'grotesque' at 25 Magdalene Street. The 17th-century building was once the Cross Keys Inn. The figure was probably a protection against witchcraft.

Folk cures and witchcraft

Any advances in 17th-century science and medicine had little effect on ordinary people. To treat the plague, for example, most townspeople relied on folk cures, herbal remedies and prayer.

Witchcraft was also widespread in the local area. There was a great fear of witches and many witch safeguards have been found in Cambridge and the surrounding villages to keep witches at bay. Sometimes, brightly coloured threads were hung in windows to 'dazzle' evil forces.

Safeguards against witches. People used to place shoes in the walls of houses to ward off witches. This shoe was found in the walls of The Three Tuns Inn on Castle Street. The patten (a wooden clog on a raised platform) was found in a house in the village of Caldecote.

Barges, bridges and stagecoaches

Navigating the Cam

Sea-going ships used to be able to sail right up the river from King's Lynn as far as Cambridge. But after Denver Sluice was completed in 1651 and the Fens drained, the river level dropped. Larger sea-going vessels now found it difficult to reach the town. Many goods had to be transferred onto smaller boats to journey further up the Cam to Quayside and beyond.

From the 17th century, it became increasingly difficult, even in small boats, to navigate the final stretch of river from Quayside to the Mill Pool. There was no continuous towpath along the Backs and the college banks were steep and high, making it virtually impossible for horses to pull barges from the riverbank. This led to the curious sight of boats being pulled along by horses, wading in the middle of the river along an underwater towpath.

The destination for much river traffic was the Mill Pool. This area was dominated by three large corn mills (see pages 68–9). The corn for the mills was grown in the fields of south Cambridgeshire, a rich grain-growing area. Enormous quantities of corn were transported to King's Lynn to be shipped on to destinations such as London.

For many hundreds of years, the River Cam was the lifeblood of Cambridge. It carried trade and prosperity to the town. It was a place for everyday activities such as washing, fishing, and disposing of waste and sewage. It also provided a vital means of power for one of Cambridge's main local industries: milling corn.

Roads in 17th and 18th century Britain were notoriously bad. Cambridge and its colleges depended on river transport for the delivery of goods, such as coal and wine, and for the export of locally-produced corn and flour. Whilst much cargo went by water, many people preferred to travel by stagecoach. The ride might be bumpier but at a speed of six miles per hour, it was quicker and more direct. The first public coach service to London started in 1653 from Devil's Tavern, on the site of the present Senate House.

Trinity Bridge. As colleges along the Backs built more low-arched bridges in the 17th and 18th centuries, it became harder for small sailing boats to use their masts and sails.

A string of barges passing Clare College. The barge at the front has lowered its sail and mast, and is being pulled by a horse.

The colleges along the Backs relied on barge deliveries for many essential provisions. Colleges used to complain that the 'coarse language' of the bargees chatting on the river interfered with the education of their 'gentlemen'.

A mailcoach guard's flintlock pistol, early 19th century.

Stand and deliver!

The 17th century was the great age of the stagecoach. From 1653, there was a regular service of stagecoaches to and from Cambridge. Numerous coaching inns, including the Hoop Hotel (on the corner of Jesus Lane and Sidney Sussex Street) provided vital 'stages' where horses could recover and passengers could rest overnight.

Stagecoaches did not travel at night for another important reason – fear of lurking highwaymen. The infamous highwayman, Dick Turpin, is said to have been a regular visitor to the town. Highwaymen frequented many of the inns along Castle Hill and Magdalene Street, ready for a quick get-away along Huntingdon Road.

Whiter than white?

The land opposite Silver Street Bridge is known as Laundress Common, part of Sheep's Green. It was so named because laundrywomen used to wash, dry and air the college laundry there. The women paid a small fee for putting up their washing posts. Stretching back as far as Peterhouse, the commonland would be transformed into a sea of white cotton sheets and shirts, flapping in the wind. Street names such as Laundress Lane and Mill Lane are a reminder of past activities in this area.

According to local legend, Dick Turpin used to hide at Ye Olde Three Tuns on Castle Street. This ancient inn, shown here in 1900, has since been pulled down.

Near Laundress Common was Newnham Mill Pool. Cows crossed the river four times a day when going between Sheep's Green and the cowsheds where they were kept. This made the riverside very muddy and covered in animal droppings. The laundry women had the unenviable task of washing and drying white sheets with filthy river water, alongside the cattle and coal horses.

Hobson's Choice

Thomas Hobson made a fortune from hiring out horses from his stables on Trumpington Street. Travellers making the long journey to London were allowed to choose a horse, so long as it was the one nearest the stable door (which was the one that was best-rested). This choice of horse – that is, no choice at all – became known as 'Hobson's choice'.

Thomas Hobson's name has entered the English language in the phrase 'Hobson's Choice'.

6 Victorian and Edwardian Cambridge

When Queen Victoria came to the throne in 1837, Cambridge was a modestly sized town with a population of just 24,000. It had a prestigious, yet old-fashioned, university, with only 800 students.

By the end of the Victorian period, Cambridge had been completely reshaped. It was a booming railway town, and had doubled in size (see map on page 57).

By 1910, at the height of the Edwardian era, the population had swelled to over 40,000. The university population had more than tripled to 3,000 students.

The University had been transformed from a finishing school for gentlemen to a modern place of study, ready to lead the world in new areas of research.

The Coronation Festival, 1838. Popular entertainments started on Midsummer Common at 5 pm. They included sack races, donkey rides, eel-dipping, and biscuit-bolting.

Marking a new era

In Cambridge, Queen Victoria's coronation was celebrated with a spectacular event for over 15,000 people. It included a gigantic feast with guests seated at 60 long tables, radiating from a rotunda where the orchestra sat. After the meal there was a hot-air balloon display and fireworks.

Queen Victoria came to the throne, a young woman of just 17. She died in 1901, a grand old lady of 82. During her reign, Cambridge doubled in population and area.

Cambridge's biggest feast ever: the Coronation Festival on Parker's Piece in June 1838. Some 7,000 joints of meat, 4,000 loaves of bread and 1,650 plum puddings were prepared for the banquet. Men had three pints (nearly two litres) of ale, women had one, and children received a half.

Boom town

In common with towns and cities all over Britain, the population in Cambridge soared in Victorian times, as people moved from the countryside to the town. In Cambridge, the population was affected by three additional things: the enclosure of open fields just outside the town; the coming of the railway; and changes in the University.

Disappearing fields

At the start of Queen Victoria's reign, most people lived in cramped housing within a mile of Cambridge's centre. The town was surrounded by a few large, open fields. These were used for farming until 1801, when Parliament passed laws allowing private landowners to exploit this land as they wished. Much of this privately owned land was then sold at a profit for housing. This took pressure off the overcrowded town centre. For the first time in more than a thousand years, the town spilled over its historic boundary, the King's Ditch, and expanded rapidly (compare with map on page 21).

Before Victoria Bridge (below) was built, in 1890, villagers from Chesterton relied on ferries to cross the river. One such ferry operated from Ferry Path, opposite the Fort St George pub. When Victoria Bridge was completed, Chesterton became much more closely linked to Cambridge.

This ferry (right), crossing the Cam between the Green Dragon pub and Stourbridge Common, was large enough to carry a horse and cart.

The railway comes to town

The new railway reached Cambridge in 1845. The town rapidly became an important railway centre, providing a convenient stop-over between London and the north. The railway industry became a major employer, boosting the population and in turn the development of residential areas. As a result, most of the land between Parker's Piece and the station was built up between 1850 and 1870, as was 'Romsey Town' from the 1880s.

An expanding University

The University also expanded rapidly from the mid-19th century. Many new college buildings sprung up to accommodate the ever-increasing number of undergraduates (including, from the 1870s, women). Three completely new colleges were set up in the 1870s and 1880s: Girton, Newnham and Selwyn.

As new subjects such as science were introduced, many new laboratories sprung up in the town centre. The vast New Museums Site, built from the 1860s, became the hub of scientific Cambridge in Victorian times.

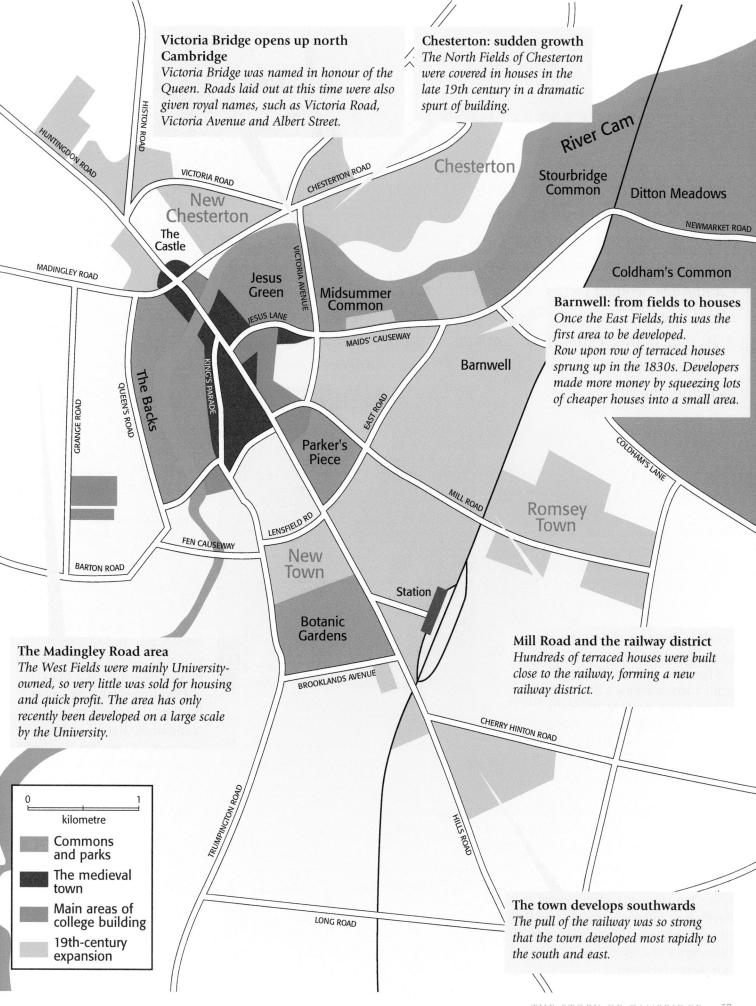

Victoria Bridge opens up north Cambridge
Victoria Bridge was named in honour of the Queen. Roads laid out at this time were also given royal names, such as Victoria Road, Victoria Avenue and Albert Street.

Chesterton: sudden growth
The North Fields of Chesterton were covered in houses in the late 19th century in a dramatic spurt of building.

HUNTINGDON ROAD

HISTON ROAD

VICTORIA ROAD

CHESTERTON ROAD

River Cam

Chesterton

Stourbridge Common

Ditton Meadows

New Chesterton

The Castle

MADINGLEY ROAD

Jesus Green

VICTORIA AVENUE

Midsummer Common

NEWMARKET ROAD

Coldham's Common

JESUS LANE

MAIDS' CAUSEWAY

Barnwell: from fields to houses
Once the East Fields, this was the first area to be developed.
Row upon row of terraced houses sprung up in the 1830s. Developers made more money by squeezing lots of cheaper houses into a small area.

GRANGE ROAD

QUEEN'S ROAD

The Backs

KING'S PARADE

Barnwell

EAST ROAD

COLDHAM'S LANE

Parker's Piece

MILL ROAD

Romsey Town

FEN CAUSEWAY

LENSFIELD RD

BARTON ROAD

New Town

Station

Mill Road and the railway district
Hundreds of terraced houses were built close to the railway, forming a new railway district.

The Madingley Road area
The West Fields were mainly University-owned, so very little was sold for housing and quick profit. The area has only recently been developed on a large scale by the University.

Botanic Gardens

BROOKLANDS AVENUE

CHERRY HINTON ROAD

TRUMPINGTON ROAD

HILLS ROAD

0	1

kilometre

Commons and parks

The medieval town

Main areas of college building

19th-century expansion

LONG ROAD

The town develops southwards
The pull of the railway was so strong that the town developed most rapidly to the south and east.

The University: time for change

By the early 19th century, the University urgently needed to improve. Much of the teaching was poor, the range of subjects was limited and many students were lazy. Catholics and Jews were barred from Cambridge, women were not even considered and few poor people could afford to go.

In spite of this, Cambridge continued to attract some brilliant scholars. From the 1840s, the University at last began to modernise and new subjects were introduced.

Many undergraduates broke the college rules. Here, one is caught with a woman in this cartoon by Moden.

Idle gentlemen and brilliant scholars

At the start of the 19th century, gentlemen-scholars were not expected to be particularly clever or hardworking. There was no entrance examination (apart from at Trinity, where one was introduced in 1836). Entrants simply had to be rich enough to pay. In fact, many undergraduates spent a lot of time just enjoying themselves – dining, drinking, hunting, shooting and gambling at the Newmarket races.

However, amongst the wealthy gentlemen-scholars, a few were also extremely talented. Many of the brightest ones studied at Trinity College, including the historian, Thomas Babington Macaulay, novelist William Thackeray and the poets George Byron and Alfred Tennyson.

Most remarkable of all the 19th-century scholars was Charles Darwin, who arrived at Christ's College in 1827 with plans to become a vicar. His carefree time at Cambridge led him – happily – to collect insects, to develop an interest in nature and then to make some of the greatest scientific discoveries that have entirely changed our view of the world.

Lord Byron: Romantic poet and hero

Lord Byron was renowned not only for his exceptional poetry, but also for his charm, wit and reckless behaviour. He went to Trinity in 1805 where, famously, he caused a stir from his very first day by bringing with him a pet bear:

I have got a new friend, the finest in the world, a tame bear. When I brought him here they [the college] asked me what I meant to do with him, and my reply was 'he should sit for a Fellowship'.

The dashing Lord Byron. He captured people's imagination all over Europe like a modern-day star.

Byron's best-known poem, *Childe Harold's Pilgrimage*, published in 1812, was rapturously received. Later, Byron took up the Greek cause in their War of Independence against the Turks. He fought bravely but died of a fever whilst in Greece in 1824, where he was mourned as a hero.

Despite his fame as a poet, his life was considered so scandalous that when his memorial statue was finished, Westminster Abbey refused to have it in Poet's Corner. It now stands in the Wren Library in Trinity.

Byron's name is remembered at the local beauty spot, Byron's Pool, where he used to enjoy an early morning dip.

New subjects to study

Traditional subjects taught at Cambridge were theology, mathematics, classics and medicine. From the 1840s, the curriculum was finally brought up-to-date. In 1848, the University set up a natural sciences tripos (a science degree). This was to have a dramatic effect on the future of Cambridge. Other new subjects soon followed, including law, history, engineering, geology, zoology and modern languages.

What is a tripos?

The final exam which leads to a degree is called a tripos. The word comes from the 15th century, when undergraduates would sit on a 'tripos', or three-legged stool, to argue their case. By the late 18th century, examinations were written rather than spoken, but the medieval name stuck.

The Botanic Garden and the new interest in science

In 1846, the Botanic Garden was opened in Trumpington Street and this is the beautiful and world-famous garden we see today. The Professor of Botany, John Henslow, managed to persuade the University to move the Gardens from their original, cramped site on Free School Lane. Here, plants had been grown as medicines since 1762.

Henslow believed passionately that the new interest in botany would lead to greater things. He was proved right. By the start of the 20th century, Cambridge scientists pioneered work on plants at the Botanics, contributing to a new branch of science – genetics.

Charles Darwin

Darwin made friends with two forward-thinking professors, John Henslow and Adam Sedgwick. This led to him being chosen as naturalist on the voyage on *HMS Beagle* to South America in 1831. Darwin's observations there led him to develop a startling new theory about evolution. In 1859 he published his controversial book, *The Origin of Species.*

Charles Darwin: a great naturalist

At Cambridge, Darwin became bored with his studies. It was while beetle-hunting in the Fens at Swaffham Bulbeck near Cambridge, that Darwin's love of natural sciences took root:

No pursuit at Cambridge was followed with nearly so much eagerness as collecting beetles... One day on tearing off some old bark, I saw two rare beetles and seized one in each hand; then I saw a third and new kind, which I could not bear to lose, so that I popped the one which I held in my right hand into my mouth. Alas it ejected some intensely acrid fluid, which burnt my tongue so that I was forced to spit the beetle out, which was lost, as well as the third one.

Beetles collected by Darwin.

The present-day Botanic Garden, set up by Charles Darwin's teacher, Henslow. Today, it is a leading university botanic garden with over 8,000 plant species.

The Fitzwilliam Museum. Like Darwin, many gentlemen at that time had a passion for collecting things. In 1816, Lord Fitzwilliam left money for a museum to house his priceless collection of paintings, prints and books. It was opened in 1848 and is now a wonderful museum of international standing.

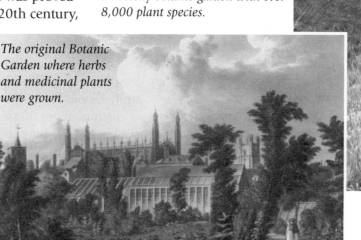

The original Botanic Garden where herbs and medicinal plants were grown.

The University: opening doors

Despite some changes in the 1840s, the University still needed to make more improvements. The traditional English universities of Oxford and Cambridge now faced stiff competition from the University of London, started in 1826.

Prince Albert was appointed Chancellor of Cambridge University in 1847. Over the next 20 years he introduced many important reforms. By the 1870s, Cambridge had finally opened its doors to students of different religions and to women.

The first five women students from Hitchin who prepared for the Cambridge tripos. They later moved to Girton, the first college for women in Cambridge.

The First Catholics and Jews

In 1856, the University at last allowed students of different religions to take degrees. This was considered very daring in Cambridge at the time. Before then, statutes dating back to Elizabeth I's reign had barred Jews and Catholics from the University. A huge Catholic Church was built for the expected flood of Catholic undergraduates. The Catholic Church of Our Lady and the English Martyrs was begun in 1885. It commemorated the Catholic martyrs – over thirty of whom had studied at Cambridge – who had died for their beliefs in the 16th and 17th centuries.

The gothic-style Catholic Church with its soaring spire is a striking local landmark.

The first married Fellows

From 1882, Fellows were at last allowed to marry. Centuries of monastic-style living came to an abrupt end. Fellows had been banned from marrying to encourage a strong, tight-knit community within the college. By the late 19th century, however, the University realised that to keep the best teachers, the ban must be lifted. This brought some surprising changes to the town as many Fellows moved out of college to live with their new wives and families. Most noticeable were the large family houses that sprung up in west Cambridge along roads such as Grange Road and West Road, and in south Cambridge along Chaucer and Latham Roads.

The first women

The idea of women studying at university was deeply shocking to many people in Victorian times. However, after a long battle, women were at last admitted to Cambridge in the 1870s. It took the determination of two women campaigners to help achieve this. In 1869, Miss Emily Davies set up the first college for women in Hitchin, about 30 miles away. She brought the women to their new college at Girton in 1873. Meanwhile, Miss Anne Jemima Clough started a small college for women in Regent Street in 1871. The women moved to Newnham College in 1875.

'This is no place for you maids'

Women were now allowed to attend lectures and take the final exams, but they could not receive degrees. They campaigned vigorously for equal rights. In 1887 and again in 1897 they pushed hard to be accepted as full members of the University, but both times lost the vote. The women faced fierce opposition, particularly from male undergraduates. Many young men plastered Cambridge with posters in huge red letters:

ADDICTED TO DANCING!

'DOWN WITH WOMEN'S DEGREES!'

BEWARE THE THIN END OF THE WEDGE! WOMEN ARE AFTER POWER TO RULE, NOT JUST EQUALITY IN DEGREES

INCAPABLE OF ACHIEVING FIRST CLASS

Despite women's progress in the 1870s, the University was the very last one in Britain to award proper degrees to women – in 1947.

Meanwhile, women persevered with great success in their own academic studies. In 1890, Philippa Fawcett of Newnham College caused a stir when she gained a higher mark than the top male graduate in mathematics, known as the 'Senior Wrangler'. The title was a tremendous honour, and until now, had always been held by a man. There were gasps of disbelief as the results were read aloud.

Feelings about women in the University ran very high. Here, a huge crowd of male undergraduates is waiting near the Senate House for the results of the ballot in 1897.

Newnham College set new standards for the University and has proudly remained an all-women college to this day. It has nurtured generations of fine scholars. These include:

Sylvia Plath, a remarkable American poet who became a Fellow at Cambridge in 1956. Whilst at Newnham she met and married Ted Hughes, also a famous poet.

Rosalind Franklin, another brilliant Newnhamite who, like Plath, died tragically young. She helped to discover the structure of DNA (see page 88).

Despite breaking new ground, the pioneer women were still constrained by the strict rules of society – as well as the college rules – of what was lady-like, and what was not. For example, female undergraduates could not attend lectures without a chaperone. One woman describes the restrictions at Newnham in 1899:

Even so, college life was very liberating for many women, especially those of a sheltered upbringing. Late evening cocoa parties were new and exciting. Women gradually broke social rules. Bicycling, for example, was considered improper for ladies, and rather daring. At first it was discouraged, but by 1896, Newnham was finally forced to build a bicycle shed!

Our long skirts, stiff collars and tight waists were very uncomfortable and even on the hockey field we were expected to have skirts below the knee. One of our team had to write home for permission to leave off her flannel petticoat when playing hockey.

M A Quiggan, 1899

Town and Gown, rich and poor

In Victorian times, many towns and cities in Britain were dominated by large industrial mills and smoky factories. But Cambridge lacked the raw materials – coal and iron – to become a major centre for manufacturing. The main source of work in 19th-century Cambridge was the University.

Cambridge was, nevertheless, sharply divided between rich and poor. Much of the wealth was concentrated in the University (the Gown), whilst many working people (the Town) struggled to make ends meet.

Kettle's Yard on Castle Hill in 1904. The area was notoriously deprived and disease-ridden. In 1851, this warren of houses was shared by nearly 120 men, women and children, working as shoemakers, dressmakers, coal porters and boatmen.

The Town

The poorest people lived in cramped dwellings above shops, in yards and down alleyways in the centre of Cambridge. Their homes rarely had running water or sewers. A newspaper describes conditions in 1850:

Pupils at St Giles near Castle Street, in 1905. The children were given free doses of Malt Extract with Cod Liver Oil to supplement their poor diet.

> In many parts of the town the dwellings of the poor are in the most disgraceful condition ... perhaps the worst of all is a place called the Falcon Yard [on Petty Cury]. In one of the houses which I visited there were 13 families residing. ...
>
> The number of persons residing in this Falcon Yard, I was informed, was about 300. There are two privies for the use of the whole of the inhabitants. Those of the inhabitants who have back windows to their rooms are in the habit of throwing all their refuse out of the windows onto a large dung-heap in the Red Lion Yard, the reeking steam from which is constantly penetrating the rooms.
>
> *Cambridge Chronicle*

From the 1880s, row upon row of terraces were built to house the town's fast-growing population. With a front parlour and individual water closets, these houses were luxurious compared with the cramped, insanitary lodgings in the centre of town.

The workhouse

If people were completely destitute, unemployed or orphaned, they ended up at the workhouse. Here, they had to work for their board and lodging. Inmates had to wear a special workhouse uniform and live to a strict regime, which included rationed food and lights out at 8 pm. Families would do anything to avoid the terrible shame of being sent to the workhouse, as well as the dread of being split up from one another.

The workhouse in Mill Road, built in 1838. The building later became the city's maternity hospital (until 1983). It now provides sheltered housing.

The contrast between rich and poor was stark. St John's College (shown here in 1851) was very wealthy. Yet it backed directly onto Kettle's Yard (left), some of the worst slums in Cambridge. In spite of this, the colleges provided vital work for many townspeople.

Giving formal dinner parties was an important social duty for the Darwin family. There was a strict etiquette to follow, including the order of who sat where around the dining table. Status was so important that the heads of colleges were even ranked according to the date their college was founded.

A Cambridge childhood

Gwen Darwin (later Raverat) was Charles Darwin's granddaughter. She described her childhood in a book, *Period Piece*, which she illustrated with beautiful drawings. Her father, George Darwin, had bought Newnham Grange – the granaries, warehouses and wharves stretching along the riverside – from the coal and corn merchants, the Beales, whose business had declined with the coming of the railways.

Gwen and her brother Charles playing 'pirates' outside Newnham Grange. It now forms part of Darwin College.

The Gown

In contrast, most colleges were very rich, and many undergraduates were from wealthy, land-owning families who could afford the college fees. In the 19th century, the number of poor students declined. The poorest scholars, once known as sizars (see page 42), used to do menial jobs in the colleges to pay for their board and lodging. This system ended as sizars were gradually replaced with paid servants.

From the 1880s, a new social group grew up in Cambridge: academic families. For the first time, Fellows were allowed to marry, move out from college rooms and set up family homes. George Darwin, son of the famous naturalist, Charles Darwin, was one of the first Fellows to do so. George Darwin was a distinguished don (university teacher) and Professor in Astronomy. The family lived at Newnham Grange and were the hub of a well-to-do academic circle. They enjoyed many Cambridge pursuits including lawn tennis, bicycle rides, boating parties and dances.

Darwin College today. It was set up in 1964. The college has wonderful views over the river.

Atoms and Apostles

In 1901, the Queen died and Edward VII came to the throne. There was a reaction to the strict manners of Victorian times, and a new relaxed attitude settled over Edwardian Cambridge. King's College in particular became known for the wild behaviour of some of its students.

Meanwhile, the University attracted some exceptional scholars and Fellows. They included scientists such as J J Thomson and Ernest Rutherford, and philosophers such as Bertrand Russell and Ludwig Wittgenstein. But tragically, many brilliant young men were to lose their lives in the First World War (see pages 72–7).

Undergraduates picnicking. Carefree outings like this were popular in Edwardian times.

The rise of science

One of the most dramatic changes in Cambridge in the late 19th century was the new interest in science. Before 1848, no science was taught in Cambridge. By 1900, natural sciences was the most popular course in the University.

In 1871 William Cavendish, Duke of Devonshire, gave money to start the Cavendish Laboratory. This was to mark the beginning of a century of stupendous achievement in science at Cambridge. The first three professors, James Clerk Maxwell, Lord Rayleigh and J J Thomson, soon gave Cambridge an international name in physics.

The atom. Rutherford suggested that electrons move round the nucleus rather like planets moving round the sun. Negative electrons are attracted to the positively charged nucleus.

Splitting the atom

In the late 19th century, scientists thought that atoms were the fundamental unit of matter and could not possibly be divided, but J J Thomson challenged this view. He discovered particles smaller than atoms which he called electrons. This led Thomson's pupil, Ernest Rutherford, to discover the nucleus.

The remarkable achievements in science came from the most basic quarters. This is the room at the Cavendish where Rutherford and Chadwick did their experiments in the 1920s.

J J Thomson discovered the electron in 1897. For this achievement, he won the Nobel Prize in 1906.

Great writers and thinkers

The intense research at the Cavendish contrasted sharply with the leisurely lifestyle that many undergraduates and Fellows enjoyed. Cycle rides and boating trips, long walks of 10 to 20 miles, 'skinny-dipping' in the river and camping at Grantchester meadows, inspired many acclaimed writers and poets, including E M Forster, Virginia Woolf and Frances Cornford (Frances Darwin before she married).

Virginia Woolf and the Bloomsbury Group

Virginia Woolf belonged to a very bright literary circle called the Bloomsbury Group. Other members included Giles Lytton Strachey, John Maynard Keynes, E M Forster, Clive and Vanessa Bell, Roger Fry and Leonard Woolf. They were influenced by the ideas of their friend and philosopher, G E Moore. Although the group was named after an area in London where they often met up, most of the members originally met to discuss books and ideas at Cambridge.

Virginia Woolf: novelist and feminist writer. One of her best-known works, 'A Room of One's Own' (1929), was based on two lectures she gave to women at Cambridge. She told them that they needed to be independent – with £50 a year and a lock on the door – to be truly creative.

Ernest Rutherford discovered the nucleus of the atom. He won the Nobel Prize in 1908.

In 1919, Rutherford also demonstrated that the nucleus contained positively charged particles called protons.

James Chadwick was, in turn, a pupil of Rutherford. In 1932 he found another particle in the nucleus, the neutron.

From this knowledge, scientists discovered that splitting a uranium nucleus started a chain reaction and tremendous energy could be released. This discovery was later put to devastating effect at Hiroshima in Japan in 1945.

Atomic power. In the last years of Victoria's reign, the first mysteries of the atom were being revealed. Within just 40 years, there was the technology to detonate the atomic bomb.

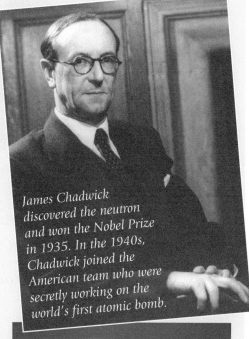

James Chadwick discovered the neutron and won the Nobel Prize in 1935. In the 1940s, Chadwick joined the American team who were secretly working on the world's first atomic bomb.

As well as nurturing writers, Cambridge – and Trinity College in particular – was fast becoming a world-famous centre for philosophy. Bertrand Russell, a brilliant philosopher and mathematician, was a Fellow at Trinity when the young Austrian philosopher, Ludwig Wittgenstein, arrived in Cambridge in 1911. Russell quickly became convinced that the man was a genius and Wittgenstein became his protégé. From 1939 to 1947 Wittgenstein was Professor of Philosophy, following another great Trinity philosopher, G E Moore.

Ludwig Wittgenstein: one of the 20th century's greatest philosophers. He is buried in this simple grave at a cemetery off Huntingdon Road.

King's College and radical students

At the turn of the 20th century, a number of undergraduates at King's challenged the social rules of the time. They included writers such as Edward Morgan Forster, who arrived at King's in 1897, and Rupert Brooke, who came up in 1906. They wore outrageous clothes and behaved in a way that the strict Victorians would have found quite shocking.

Members of King's challenged the intellectual ideas, as well as the social rules of the day. The economist John Maynard Keynes, for example, had a great impact not only on Britain's economic policy, but also in world affairs. His ideas directly influenced President Roosevelt's New Deal in the USA in 1932.

The Cambridge Apostles

The Apostles is a famous and secret debating society. Its members are elected for life. The society was started in 1820 and early members included the poet Lord Tennyson. The Apostles had a particularly brilliant period in Edwardian times, when many topics such as religion were furiously discussed. In nearly 200 years, members have included eminent politicians, writers, scientists – and even infamous spies such as Anthony Blunt! (See page 83.)

Some famous members of the Apostles in Edwardian times were:

Rupert Brooke (poet)
E M Forster (novelist)
G E Moore (philosopher)
J M Keynes (economist)
Bertrand Russell (philosopher)
Giles Lytton Strachey (writer)
Ludwig Wittgenstein (philosopher)

Rupert Brooke in 1915. Both his exceptional good looks and his poetry were legendary. He attracted a considerable following at Grantchester.

John Maynard Keynes: a great 20th-century economist. He argued that the catastrophic depression in America in the early 1930s could be cured by creating lots of jobs for the unemployed.

E M Forster visiting his old college. Like Keynes, Forster was deeply affected by his time at King's. He became one of England's leading writers, best known for 'A Passage to India'. An earlier novel 'Maurice', written in 1913, was largely set in Cambridge.

'But Grantchester! Ah, Grantchester!'

In the early 20th century, many undergraduates were drawn to the peaceful charm of the village of Grantchester, just a few miles from Cambridge. In particular, the poet Rupert Brooke fell in love with the place and made the village nationally famous.

Brooke won a scholarship to King's College and in 1913 became a Fellow. He lodged in Grantchester, first at Orchard House and then at the Old Vicarage, where he enjoyed a relaxed, bohemian lifestyle, walking around the village barefoot and swimming naked in the river by moonlight. One day, Maynard Keynes visited Brooke at Grantchester and found him 'sitting in the midst of admiring females with nothing on but an embroidered sweater'. This would have been considered very daring at the time!

Brooke remembered Grantchester longingly from abroad in his well-known poem *The Old Vicarage*:

The Old Vicarage at Grantchester, where Brooke once lived. It later became home to another writer, Jeffrey Archer, who made millions from writing best-sellers.

Ah God! to see the branches stir
Across the moon at Grantchester!
To smell the thrilling-sweet and rotten
Unforgettable, unforgotten
River-smell, and hear the breeze
Sobbing in the little trees.
Say, do the elm-clumps greatly stand
Still guardians of that holy land?
...
And laughs the immortal river still
Under the mill, under the mill?
Say, is there Beauty yet to find?
And Certainty? and Quiet kind?
Deep meadows yet, for to forget
The lies, and truths, and pain? ... oh! yet
Stands the Church clock at ten to three?
And is there honey still for tea?

Grantchester has continued to inspire many artists and writers since Rupert Brooke. These are the words of a song by Pink Floyd, the world-famous rock band who started out from Cambridge in the 1960s:

Grantchester Meadows today.

Grantchester Meadows

... See the splashing of the kingfisher
   flashing to the water
And a river of green is sliding unseen
   beneath the trees
Laughing as it passes through the
   endless summer
Making for the sea.
In the lazy water meadow I lay down
All around me golden sun flakes settle
   on the ground
Basking in the sunshine of a bygone
   afternoon
Bringing sounds of yesterday into this
   city room.

Today, the tea gardens at Orchard House seem to present a timeless summer scene. Yet the Orchard also broke with Victorian social rules when, in 1897, a group of students asked for their tea to be served in the rambling apple orchard behind the house, rather than on the formal front lawn. The Orchard still serves afternoon teas in this idyllic setting beneath the apple trees.

The Orchard tea gardens in full blossom in 1910. Rupert Brooke drew an impressive crowd of regulars here, including Bertrand Russell, E M Forster, Virginia Woolf, J M Keynes and the artist Augustus John.

River work, river fun

From the mid-19th century, the Cam began to change from a working river to a place of leisure. There were two reasons for this. First, it was much cheaper to use the new railway for haulage, so trade declined on the Cam. Secondly, the river water – contaminated for so long with sewage and rubbish – was finally cleaned up. Pleasure boating now began!

The King's and Bishop's Mills in the 1890s. The site of the present-day weir is just visible to the left.

The same view today. The mills were demolished in 1928. The Mill pub is on the left.

From water wheels to steam power

For over 900 years, the town had been a centre of milling. The town's three main corn mills at the Mill Pool and Newnham Pool were powered by river water. It turned large wooden water wheels and the heavy grinding stones that milled the corn into flour. A few reminders of this milling heyday survive by the Mill Pool: the rushing water in the mill races (channels to the old water wheels); and a short strip of cobbled road where loading and unloading once took place.

The Mill Pool changed dramatically when the Bishop's Mill and King's Mill were combined and converted to steam power in the mid-19th century. Sitting by the peaceful weir today, it is hard to imagine that this was once the site of two deafening steam- and water-powered grinding mills, each producing thousands of kilos of flour every week.

A cleaner river

In early Victorian times, the river was a stinking open sewer. Between Magdalene Bridge and Barnwell, the untreated sewage of thousands of people living near the river was simply poured in. Diseases such as typhoid and cholera were particular dangers. The problem was made more acute as the population was growing so fast.

Not all Cambridge's waste went into the river, though. Much of it was collected from household privies in the 'honey wagon', and this night soil was spread on the open fields of Cambridge as manure. But by the 19th century, the honey wagon was completely overwhelmed and the state of the river was desperate. Finally, in 1895, proper drains were installed. Underground sewers led to the new steam pumping station built at Cheddar's Lane. Here, all the town's refuse was collected and burnt, to fuel the engines that pumped the town's sewage under the river to Milton.

Watermill country

Further upstream from the Newnham Mill Pool, the river became narrower, shallower and more difficult to navigate. Nonetheless, some boats did continue the journey beyond Cambridge. This quieter stretch of river landscape was known as 'watermill country' because there were many small, ancient mills. The last one in the river valley, Harston Mill, was finally closed in 1964.

'We are not amused.' Whilst on a visit to Cambridge, Queen Victoria asked the Master of Trinity why there were so many pieces of paper floating in the river. 'Those, ma'am, are notices to say that bathing is forbidden', he cleverly replied.

The river declines

In the mid-19th century the town's mills were still important enough that the new railway companies wanted to build their stations nearby. In 1846, for example, the Cambridge–Oxford Railway wanted to place a station on Silver Street. The University refused and the railway was built off Hills Road instead. Cut off from the new means of transport, the riverside mills could no longer make a profit and so fell into terminal decline. The hythe just below Magdalene Bridge was the last commercial quay to survive (see page 22). As the railways took business away from the river, Quayside became nearly deserted. The run-down area was redeveloped in 1989, and Quayside is now busy once more, this time with pleasure boats.

Pleasure craft and swimming

With less river traffic and cleaner water, swimming and boating became increasingly popular in Victorian times. People preferred to swim 'up river' at Sheep's Green and Coe Fen where the water was cleanest. Gwen Raverat describes the hazards of a popular summer activity, a boating trip up river:

All summer, Sheep's Green and Coe Fen were pink with boys, as naked as God made them; for bathing drawers did not exist then; or, at least, not on Sheep's Green. Now to Up River, the goal of all the best picnics, the boats had to go right by the bathing places. These dangerous straits were taken in silence, and at full speed.

Gwen Raverat, *Period Piece: A Cambridge Childhood*, 1952

The old mill at Grantchester was a working mill, run by the Nutter family who had a century-long history of milling in the town. It was burnt down in a dramatic blaze in 1928.

The mill was then rebuilt (below). The original medieval mill pool would have been well-stocked with fish and eels. The miller used to supply eels to the colleges for special feast days.

Rowing: a new sport

In the 19th century, many sports were developed at Oxford and Cambridge, including rowing. The Cambridge University Boat Club began in 1827, and the first boat race against Oxford was held just two years later on the River Thames. Today, the annual Boat Race is still fiercely fought between Cambridge and Oxford, watched by millions world-wide on television. The crews are distinguished by their traditional colours: light blue for Cambridge; dark blue for Oxford.

Another popular rowing event is the Bumping Races, or 'Bumps', started in Cambridge in 1828. College crews chase other crews on the river, aiming to touch the boat in front. If they succeed, they swap places in the next day's race. This unusual form of racing developed because the river was too narrow for crews to race side by side.

The Bumps today. Huge crowds gather to watch the four-day event on the Cam.

The railway

In 1845, the railway came to Cambridge and the town changed for ever. The new railway meant quicker journeys and cheaper fares for everyone. Stagecoaches were forced out of business. River traffic on the Cam declined too as the railways competed for freight. Between 1870 and 1900 the town grew enormously as the railway flourished.

Great Eastern steam locomotive at Cambridge Station, 1866.

The railway arrives

The first steam train pulled into Cambridge station in July 1845 to a cheering crowd. The line had been built by a private company, the Eastern Counties Railway, and it ran from the East End of London. The Great Northern Railway built a competing line from London King's Cross in 1866.

Cambridge station was built some distance from the town centre. This had been at the University's insistence, and reflected the power the University had – and still has – in Cambridge. The University did not want the station within a mile of any of its buildings, fearing it would be too noisy and would distract its students.

The first station, built in 1845, soon needed enlarging. It was rebuilt in 1863 and this is the fine arcaded building we see today. The present station has an unusual claim to fame. Its platform, which stretches for nearly a quarter of a mile, is the longest platform in Europe!

The original station in 1845. Its out-of-town location meant good business for the hansom cabs and horse-drawn omnibuses.

The impact of the railway

Some stagecoach companies were affected almost at once by the new railway. For example, one company had to sell 500 horses within two weeks of the railway's opening. Within just four years, the last stagecoach left Cambridge for London.

In the long run, though, Cambridge benefited greatly from its new rail links. For centuries, heavy goods had been carried by boat, but from the 1860s, freight was carried much more cheaply and quickly by rail. For passengers, travel by road had been arduous and slow. The journey to London by stagecoach, for example, usually took two days, allowing time for the horses to rest. The same 57-mile journey now took just under two hours by train.

As the river trade declined, Foster Brothers, who owned all three riverside mills at that time, built a new flour mill near the station in 1894. It is still one of the largest buildings in the city. They also built Fosters' Bank, an impressive Victorian landmark in Sidney Street (and now the Lloyds TSB Bank) for their mill workers to use.

The railway had a dramatic effect on the size of the town too. As train traffic increased, there were more and more jobs on the railways, and newcomers flooded in. By 1884, the census showed that over half the people living in Cambridge's 'Romsey Town' were born outside Cambridge, and drawn to the town for work.

At first, many railwaymen lived in the new terraced houses built along roads such as Panton Street and Russell Street, in an area still known as 'New Town'. From the 1870s, a thriving railway community sprung up in 'Sturton Town' off Mill Road, and another in 'Romsey Town'.

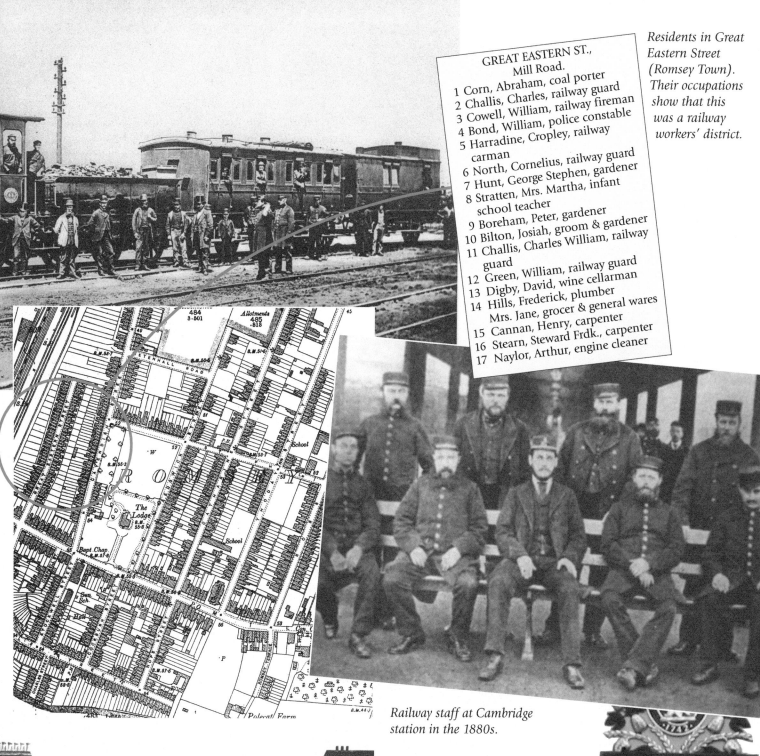

GREAT EASTERN ST.,
Mill Road.
1 Corn, Abraham, coal porter
2 Challis, Charles, railway guard
3 Cowell, William, railway fireman
4 Bond, William, police constable
5 Harradine, Cropley, railway
  carman
6 North, Cornelius, railway guard
7 Hunt, George Stephen, gardener
8 Stratten, Mrs. Martha, infant
  school teacher
9 Boreham, Peter, gardener
10 Bilton, Josiah, groom & gardener
11 Challis, Charles William, railway
  guard
12 Green, William, railway guard
13 Digby, David, wine cellarman
14 Hills, Frederick, plumber
  Mrs. Jane, grocer & general wares
15 Cannan, Henry, carpenter
16 Stearn, Steward Frdk., carpenter
17 Naylor, Arthur, engine cleaner

Residents in Great Eastern Street (Romsey Town). Their occupations show that this was a railway workers' district.

Railway staff at Cambridge station in the 1880s.

Mill Road in 1901.

Modern-day pub signs such as the Locomotive and the Beaconsfield recall links with Romsey's Victorian and railway past.

The Jubilee: built in Queen Victoria's Jubilee Year, 1887

The Empress: also built in 1887.

7 Cambridge at war

The Cambridge War Memorial on Hills Road, erected in 1919. The statue shows a young soldier returning from war, looking back over his shoulder towards the station, from where so many had set off.

The two world wars of the 20th century had an enormous impact on the town and University of Cambridge. The First World War (1914–18) was seen at the time as 'the war to end all wars'. Yet within a generation, the men of Cambridgeshire set off once more to fight in the Second World War (1939–45).

The First World War

When war was declared, many men from Cambridge rushed to join the army. They set off to France in an optimistic and patriotic mood, but this began to change as they saw more and more of their colleagues fall in the trenches.

As news of the terrible fatalities started to arrive, Cambridge suffered twice over. Not only did a large number of townsmen lose their lives, but also a great many Cambridge undergraduates from all over the country. These college men, many of them fresh from school, were recruited as officers. They suddenly found themselves leading soldiers in the most terrifying conditions. A generation of young scholars was decimated by the war.

A recruitment poster from the First World War urging men to enlist.

Soldiers departing in 1939. As they march past, they salute the memorial to those who died in the Great War. The names of those killed in the Second World War were added on later.

Undergraduates carry their gas masks and helmets to lectures.

A low-flying Spitfire photographed from the ground in 1943.

The Second World War

The carnage was to happen all over again just two decades later. In 1939, Hitler invaded Poland, triggering the Second World War. All men between 18 and 40 were conscripted for military service.

People on the home front were also deeply affected by the conflict. Cambridge was fortunate that it was not a main target for German bombing raids. However, townspeople felt the nearness of the conflict as RAF warplanes flew from the local airfields on their bombing raids to mainland Europe.

The First World War

When the First World War began, hundreds of eager recruits lined up at the Corn Exchange to join the army. Many were just 19, and some even younger. Within days, the town was transformed as young men became soldiers; parks and commons became fields of tents; and black academic gowns were swapped for khaki uniforms.

Once they reached the trenches in France, the full horror of trench warfare became all too apparent. At the Battle of the Somme in 1916 over 20,000 British men were killed in just one day of fighting. Thousands of injured soldiers were sent home, and Cambridge became a major clearing-station for the casualties.

Your King & Country need you.

A CALL TO ARMS.

AN addition of 100,000 men to His Majesty's Regular Army is immediately necessary in the present grave National Emergency.

Lord Kitchener is confident that this appeal will be at once responded to by all those who have the safety of our Empire at heart.

TERMS OF SERVICE.

General Service for a period of 3 years or until the war is concluded.

Age of enlistment between 19 and 30.

HOW TO JOIN.

Full information can be obtained at any Post Office in the Kingdom or at any Military Depot.

God Save the King.

The trenches were good for defence, but made attack almost impossible. Soldiers ordered to 'go over the top' of the trench faced enemy machine-gun fire, shelling, tangled barbed wire and a sea of mud.

It was Lord Kitchener's job to persuade men to join up. Advertisements appeared in the local press, including this one in the Cambridge Daily News, 21 August 1914.

Soldiers camping on Parker's Piece, August 1914. Vast camps were also set up on Grantchester Meadows and Midsummer Common, where hundreds of white tents were pitched and army horses grazed.

Cambridge in khaki

This was among the first conflicts in which British soldiers wore khaki as camouflage. Army uniforms became a new, yet familiar sight all over Cambridge. The Sixth Division was billeted (lodged) in the town, taking over every space available, before setting off to France.

In October, at the start of the new university term, the lecture halls were eerily deserted. Colleges emptied as over half the undergraduates signed up to fight. Many of the colleges were then filled with billeted soldiers and nurses.

At the Front

Thousands of men set off by train from Cambridge station to the front line in northern France – destination unknown – and expecting to return within a few months. They were completely unprepared for the ordeal that lay ahead. Both sides dug themselves into trenches that faced each other, stretching for mile upon mile.

The war reached deadlock in 1915. The year 1916 was a turning point: the pace of killing meant that even more soldiers were needed. The British government introduced conscription, so men now *had* to join the army.

Rupert Brooke: war poet

Rupert Brooke was a Fellow at Cambridge (see pages 66–7). Eager to fight for his country, he joined up as an officer in 1914. He died near Gallipoli in 1915.

Brooke became very famous for his wartime poems in which he expressed a romantic ideal of war. These lines are from one of the best-known poems in the English language. At the time, many people who had lost loved ones found comfort in its patriotism.

The Soldier

If I should die, think only this of me:
That there's some corner of a foreign field
That is for ever England. There shall be
In that rich earth a richer dust concealed;
A dust whom England bore, shaped, made aware,
Gave, once, her flowers to love, her ways to roam,
A body of England's breathing English air,
Washed by the rivers, blest by suns of home.

First verse of the Sonnet, 1914

These men from the Fens were experts at digging drainage ditches. Their skills were now put to a grim new use – digging miles of trenches and tunnels on the Western Front.

The wounded return

From early in the war, there was a
continuous flood of casualties arriving
in Cambridge. The hospital wards were
soon overwhelmed with victims of
shell-shock, shrapnel wounds, mustard
gas attacks and trench foot.

   Cambridge was an obvious place for
a clearing-station. It had a ready supply
of well-trained doctors and nurses at
Addenbrooke's Hospital, and excellent
railway links to bring the wounded
home. There were not enough beds at
Addenbrooke's, though, so the First
Eastern General Hospital was set up as
an army hospital. Many VADs
(Voluntary Aid Detachments)
volunteered to help the regular nurses
with the casualties.

*Arriving at Cambridge station. Wounded
soldiers lifted by stretcher from the train and
taken by ambulance to hospital.*

*The old Addenbrooke's Hospital (now the
Judge Institute of Management Studies). In
1914 the children's ward was converted into a
ward for wounded soldiers. Situated
inconveniently on the top floor, it was nicknamed Tipperary Ward because, in the words
of the popular wartime song, 'It's a long way
to Tipperary'.*

Temporary beds at the First Eastern

The First Eastern General Hospital was
set up in various sites across town.
During the summer holidays of 1914,
the Leys, a public school in Cambridge,
was turned into a fully working
hospital, complete with operating
theatre. The cloisters of Trinity College
also provided hospital accommodation,
with 250 tightly packed beds beneath
the arches in Nevile's Court. Another
hospital was set up at King's and Clare
Cricket Ground (now the site of the
University Library). It had row upon
row of pre-fabricated huts for over
1,000 patients.

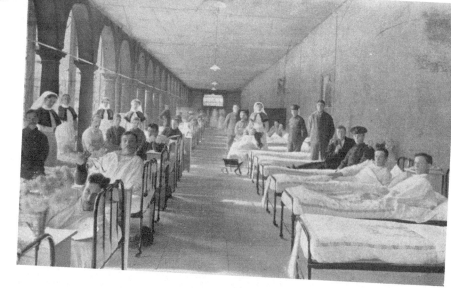

*One of the temporary wards at Trinity College. A wooden floor was added as the
original stone paving was too bumpy.*

The First Eastern was renowned as an open-air hospital. The fresh air helped recovery and prevented infections from spreading. A nurse describes working there:

Theoretically open air is great; in practice, after a winter spell on night duty there, I could wish all theorists a like experience. Chilblains? Bootsful of 'em. We make for ourselves cunning places of retreat, with screens and rugs... There we sit and watch while Tommy [a British soldier] snores in ten different keys. Sometimes he has a nightmare, thinks he is again charging the Huns [the Germans], or has lost his company and can't find it, and we tap him gently on the arm to remind him that he is no longer at war.

First Eastern General Hospital Gazette, 1915

The temporary hospital at King's and Clare Cricket Ground. Patients wore a bright blue uniform with a red tie so that they could be easily spotted in the hospital grounds. The army was afraid patients might try to escape to avoid being sent back to the Front.

The war wounded were very well cared for. Between 1914 and 1918 over 62,000 patients passed through the First Eastern; 437 died.

Campaigning for peace

Most people strongly supported the war effort, but some people believed Britain should not be fighting under any circumstances. In 1916, when conscription was introduced, those who refused to fight were known as Conscientious Objectors. They were branded as traitors and cowards, and could be imprisoned.

It took a lot of courage to campaign for peace but one Cambridge don in particular, Bertrand Russell, did speak out. He was a brilliant philosopher who could argue cleverly and this made him seem even more of a threat. In 1916, the government prosecuted him for a leaflet he wrote, defending a conscientious objector. Russell was sent to prison for six months and sacked from Trinity in 1916. He was not invited back to Cambridge until 1944.

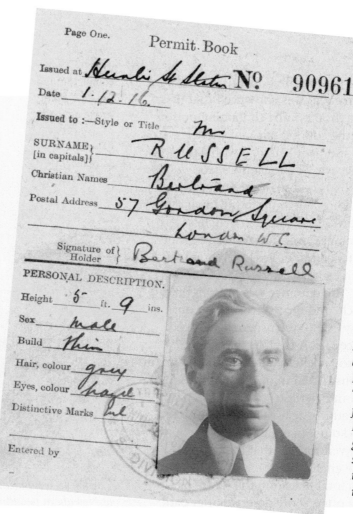

Peace campaigner, Bertrand Russell. This is a page from his Permit Book. The government stopped him from travelling freely in Britain.

The Second World War

As soon as war was declared in September 1939, people feared that Germany would start bombing cities such as London and Portsmouth. With their large weapons factories and docks, they were obvious targets. Cambridge was not a main target, but there were many local airfields, such as Duxford and Fowlmere, which drew German bombers to the Cambridge area. Throughout the war, the roar of RAF (Royal Air Force) planes overhead was a familiar sound across the skies of East Anglia.

For security reasons, the Cambridge Daily News did not name the street or town of this bomb damage in January 1941. But the location was easily recognisable to local people as Mill Road.

Bombs and blackouts

Preparations for war on the home front began in 1938. The government was convinced that the Germans would drop bombs containing poison gas. So all over the country, air-raid shelters were hastily erected, and people issued with gas masks.

In Cambridge, every conceivable space was transformed into air-raid shelters. A number of large public shelters were built in the town centre, including one on Christ's Pieces. Trenches were dug on Midsummer Common. A maze of wine cellars that stretched under Peas Hill, originally built for an 18th century inn, were also used to provide shelter. The entrance was in front of St Edward's Church, and nearly every night during the war as many as 250 townspeople climbed down into the cellars. As well as the public shelters, Anderson shelters were delivered to many homes to be constructed in back gardens. A few still stand, now in a perilous state of disrepair.

Another precaution against the bombing was the nightly blackout. Street lights remained unlit throughout the war for fear that the lighting might guide the enemy planes. With strict petrol rationing and a total blackout, the centre of Cambridge was often eerily deserted after dark.

Concrete-lined trenches taking shape on Midsummer Common in March 1939.

*Gas masks were meant to be carried at **all** times. Here, children at Newnham paddling pool are showing how to be really prepared!*

Despite these precautions, the first bombs to fall on Cambridge hit some houses in Vicarage Terrace on 19 June 1940, killing 10 people. Other air raids in Cambridge occurred when German planes off-loaded surplus bombs before flying back across the Channel. In total, 1,600 high-explosive bombs fell in the Cambridge area, 30 people were killed, and 70 injured.

The evacuees arrive in Cambridge

To escape the heavy bombing in large cities, many children were evacuated to smaller towns and villages for safety. Most evacuees arriving in Cambridge came from Tottenham and Islington in London. Not all evacuees were happy with their new homes. By January 1940, after just three months, nearly half the evacuees had returned to London, preferring to face the terror of the Blitz than to stay a day longer in Cambridge.

These are some of the evacuees' comments:

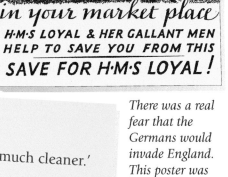

Imagine this in Cambridge

Imagine this in your market place
H·M·S LOYAL & HER GALLANT MEN HELP TO SAVE YOU FROM THIS
SAVE FOR H·M·S LOYAL!

There was a real fear that the Germans would invade England. This poster was designed to shock people into supporting the war effort.

'Cambridge people in most cases are snobs.'
Girl aged 14

'I like Cambridge better than London because it is much cleaner.'
Girl aged 9

'I miss the wide highways and the careful drivers of London. The streets here are too narrow, the town streets are too crowded by parked cars.'
Boy aged 14

'I also miss the enclosed swimming baths we have in London. I do *not* like the dirty rivers in which the people of Cambridge have to swim.'
Boy aged 14

Evacuees flooding into Cambridge. Over 3,000 children came by train from London in September 1939.

Fighter pilots and bombing raids

Cambridge lay right in the heart of 'bomber country'. The area was ideal for the Royal Air Force. It was flat, quite sparsely populated and near to enemy territory. Heavy bomber planes regularly took off from airfields such as Bourn and Oakington. Smaller fighter planes, such as Spitfires, flew from bases including Fowlmere and Duxford.

The Battle of Britain

In June 1940, Britain was in a particularly desperate situation. France had surrendered to Germany, and Hitler was now planning to invade Britain. As large formations of German planes roared over the Channel to blast RAF airfields in East Anglia and bombard British cities, the RAF pilots took off in Spitfires and Hurricanes to face them in battle. This period of fierce fighting in the air became known as the 'Battle of Britain'. In the fighting, the Germans lost over 1,700 planes; the British just over 900. The Germans gave up their immediate plans to invade.

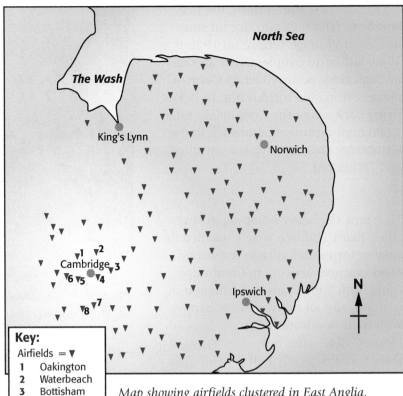

Key:
Airfields = ▼
1 Oakington
2 Waterbeach
3 Bottisham
4 Cambridge (Teversham)
5 Lord's Bridge
6 Bourn
7 Duxford
8 Fowlmere

Map showing airfields clustered in East Anglia.

Douglas Bader: fighter pilot

The legendary RAF pilot, Douglas Bader, regularly flew from Duxford during the war. He had already lost both his legs in a near-fatal flying accident in 1931. Yet Bader persuaded the RAF to let him fly again. In 1940 he led a formation of five squadrons from Duxford – his famous Big Wing – which shot down many German Messerschmitts.

In 1941 Bader's Spitfire was hit. In a miraculous escape, he parachuted to safety. Luckily, his artificial legs were detachable as his right leg became trapped and was left behind in the plane wreckage. Bader was captured by the Germans and later imprisoned in the notorious prison camp at Colditz.

Bader climbing into his Spitfire at Duxford.

Children at Milton Road Primary School collecting scrap metal. When war broke out, Britain urgently needed more weapons and planes. People willingly supported appeals such as the Spitfire Fund, to collect scrap metal to melt down for arms.

Spitfires were fast, streamlined fighter planes. Today, Duxford is a famous air museum where restored Spitfires often take to the skies in spectacular air displays.

Pilots in town

Pilots from the nearby air bases filled the pubs of Cambridge and the surrounding villages. They were easily recognisable in their blue RAF uniforms. Many were raw recruits who had only recently left school, and had little training or flying experience. On average, a fighter pilot could expect to survive for just one month. A young pilot remembers a night out in Cambridge:

The Eagle attracted many young pilots during the war. Inside the pub, the air would be thick with cigarette smoke, the windows covered with heavy blackout curtains.

That evening, as usual, we went to the pubs; the Blue Boar, the Mitre, Joe Mullins', the Bath, the Eagle. The night throbbed with aircraft. The bars were blue with RAF.

Surrounded by 'wings' [qualified aircraft pilots wearing the insignia of wings] and DFCs [pilots awarded the Distinguished Flying Cross], we were painfully aware of our insignificance. But sometimes in the midst of all the noise and laughter, a man in blue would sit, slowly sipping beer. From the stripes on his sleeve our envious looks would slide upward to the 'wings' and the purple/white slashes of the DFC, and up. Then came the shock: the schoolboy face, the greyish skin, the acne, the old lines around the eyes, staring vacantly from dark, deep sockets.

Many pilots scorched their names on the ceiling of the Eagle pub with candle flames. The original wartime graffiti can still be seen today. Squadron 222, based at Duxford, was one of many that left its mark.

Frank Whittle: inventor of the jet

The battle for supremacy in the air was matched by a fierce race between Britain and Nazi Germany to develop the first jet-powered plane.

It was Frank Whittle, a brilliant RAF engineer and Cambridge student, who first came up with the idea of the high-speed jet engine. This would replace the piston engine and propeller of existing planes. Whittle told the Air Ministry of his ingenious plans, but it was only when he went to study at Peterhouse, in 1933, that his invention was taken seriously.

In 1938, with war looming, the Air Ministry finally give Whittle the funding he needed. He tested

The Meteor, the first jet propelled aircraft to be used in action by the Royal Air Force. It's two Derwent engines, were a direct development from Whittle's invention which has transformed our world and made possible the high-speed jets we have today.

his jet plane in Britain's first jet-powered flight in 1941. But due to the Air Ministry's earlier lack of support, it was Germany, not Britain, who produced the first jet fighter – the Heinkel He 178 – in 1939.

After the war, Whittle felt very bitter and let down. He gave up all rights to his invention. In 1948, his achievements were at last recognised and he was knighted.

From World War to Cold War

In 1941, Japanese planes bombed Pearl Harbor and this incident brought the Americans into the war. Their impact was soon felt on both the fighting and home fronts. Two million Americans flooded into Britain and many settled in airbases in East Anglia. They brought optimism and fresh life to the area in the drab and dreary war years. In 1945, Nazi Germany was finally defeated.

After the war, a new era of 'Cold War' began. There was a period of deep suspicion and fear between East and West Europe. Cambridge played a crucial part in this Cold War era, which lasted from 1945 until 1989 (when Germany was finally re-united).

The Americans enjoyed leave from their airbases, often visiting Cambridge. From 1943, GIs (American servicemen) became a familiar sight in the town.

American pilots in East Anglia

In 1943, Duxford and other airfields in the area were completely handed over to the US Airforce (USAAF). Local people became accustomed to a new sight in the skies – the distinctive black-and-white checkerboard markings of American planes. The USAAF generally bombed by day, whilst the RAF went out at night. In their final mission, the Duxford US fighter pilots escorted the RAF bombers which blasted Hitler's mountain hideout, Berchtesgaden, in April 1945.

At first, the American visitors were regarded as a curiosity, with their different manners and accents. The English drank endless cups of tea whilst the Americans enjoyed coffee and doughnuts. The Americans brought with them food and drink such as coke, chewing gum and peanut butter that very few people here had tasted before. These were particularly tantalising in war-rationed, sugar-deprived Britain.

The Bull Hotel on Trumpington Street was used as an American headquarters during the war.

What did the Americans think of life here? They liked the polite British manners, and the English pubs and beer. But they remembered other aspects too:

> I have to admit that the thing that struck me most after my first journey on an English bus was the smell. It stank and so did the people.
>
> *Sgt Irving Shapiro, 94th Bomb Group*

To recover and relax after dangerous flying missions, pilots enjoyed activities such as American football and basketball. Station dances brought in hordes of young women from the surrounding towns and villages, including Cambridge. At the bases, women picked up the latest new dance from the States: the 'jitterbug'. Many romances blossomed. During the war, at least 135 Duxford GIs married local women.

Cambridge code-breakers

Even after the Americans had joined the war, victory was far from certain. Britain and the Allies desperately needed to crack the Nazis' secret code to discover where Hitler would strike next. The Nazis' cypher was produced on a machine called Enigma, an ingenious coding device.

In 1939, code-breakers from all over the country were ordered in total secrecy to its intelligence headquarters – Station X – at Bletchley Park. Many of them were brilliant scholars recruited from Cambridge, including Alan Turing, a Fellow at King's and Gordon Welchman, a Fellow at Sidney Sussex. They worked day and night and finally succeeded in breaking the code. This helped to shorten the war, and so saved countless lives.

American losses

Tragically, many Americans lost their lives in the war. They are remembered at the American War Cemetery in Madingley, near Cambridge. This is the only Second World War burial ground in Britain. The 30 acres of land was a gift to the USA from the University of Cambridge. The cemetery was officially opened in June 1944.

The American War Cemetery. The field of nearly 4,000 white headstones is a reminder of the tremendous US contribution to the war. There are also 5,000 names of those missing in action, inscribed on a long, monumental wall.

Celebrating VE Day (Victory in Europe) in Thoday Street.

Victory at last

On 8 May 1945, Europe celebrated VE Day and the people of Cambridge joined in the celebrations. But for many families in the area, the war was far from over. In 1942 the Cambridgeshire battalions had been sent to help defend Singapore. Many had been captured by the Japanese. Not until August 1945 did Japan finally surrender too.

After nearly four years away, the British prisoners-of-war who returned were barely recognisable. They had been forced to work on the 'Railway of Death' from Thailand to Burma, where they suffered horribly from exhaustion, starvation and disease. Nearly 800 'Cambridgeshires' never came home at all.

Cambridge and the Cold War

From 1945, during the Cold War, there was a real fear that the Soviet Union (Russia) might attack Britain and the West, and there would be a completely devastating nuclear war. In case of war, the government had secret plans to divide the country into regions, each with a purpose-built War Room. Cambridge was one of the 12 regional headquarters, along with cities such as London, Nottingham and Reading. In the Cambridge region, war would have been conducted from a purpose-built concrete bunker off Brooklands Avenue. This secret bunker, built in 1952, was designed to withstand nuclear attack. It can still be seen, overgrown with ivy, from Hobson's Brook near Trumpington Road.

Cambridge Spies

The 'Cambridge five' were all bright undergraduates and four of the five went to Trinity. Like many intellectuals at that time, they were attracted to the ideals of Communist Russia. Whilst at Cambridge, they were recruited as spies by the KGB (the Russian Intelligence Service). Three joined in 1934: Guy Burgess, Donald Maclean and Kim Philby. Two more joined the group in 1937: Anthony Blunt and John Cairncross.

They were brilliantly successful as spies. Burgess and Maclean went to work at the British Foreign Office where they leaked state secrets to the Russians. They came under suspicion and had to flee to Moscow in 1951. The charming and masterly spy Kim Philby, who joined the British Secret Service, was the 'third man' who had to flee in 1961. In 1964, Blunt secretly confessed he was a spy too. Later, the 'fifth man', Cairncross, was also revealed as a spy.

8 Modern Cambridge

In the last 100 years, Cambridge has grown tremendously in size, population and wealth. Cambridge is now one of the most prosperous and fast-growing cities in Britain.

Today, Cambridge stretches right out towards the A14 and M11 – major roads that almost completely encircle the city. At its heart, though, Cambridge remains recognisably medieval. Its narrow streets follow an ancient pattern, centred on the river and Market Place. The colleges, Backs and commonland create a timeless scene in the rapidly changing city.

Bicycles are often the quickest way to get around the congested city. Cambridge prides itself on being traffic-free in the very centre, long before many other cities.

Cows grazing on commonland just a few hundred metres from the city centre. The commons are lush, marshy river meadows where cattle have grazed for hundreds of years. They are easily flooded when the river swells, so the land remains undeveloped.

A booming hi-tech city

The population in Cambridge doubled during the 20th century. In 1901 the population was 38,000. In 2001 it was 109,000. It continues to grow at four times the national rate in the 21st century. The city has grown spectacularly since the late 1960s, largely because of the boom in hi-tech industry. Many highly skilled people have moved to Cambridge for work, swelling the population and boosting the local economy.

Expanding city and the Green Belt

Since the 1960s, the University has expanded rapidly to the south and west of Cambridge whilst the Town has pushed to the north and east. However, Cambridge cannot grow any more because it is restricted by a band of land called the Green Belt.

This Green Belt was put in place in the 1950s to stop the city from sprawling. In this respect it has been very successful. The people of Cambridge are lucky to have countryside just a few miles from the city centre. However, the downside is that there are not enough houses for people working in the city, and little space to build more. Many people are forced to live in the surrounding villages and to drive into work. For example, over half the population of the villages of Milton and Bar Hill commute into the city. This causes much traffic congestion on roads into the city.

In the 21st century, one of the greatest challenges is to provide new homes for working people – and ones that they can afford. Public transport urgently needs to be improved too.

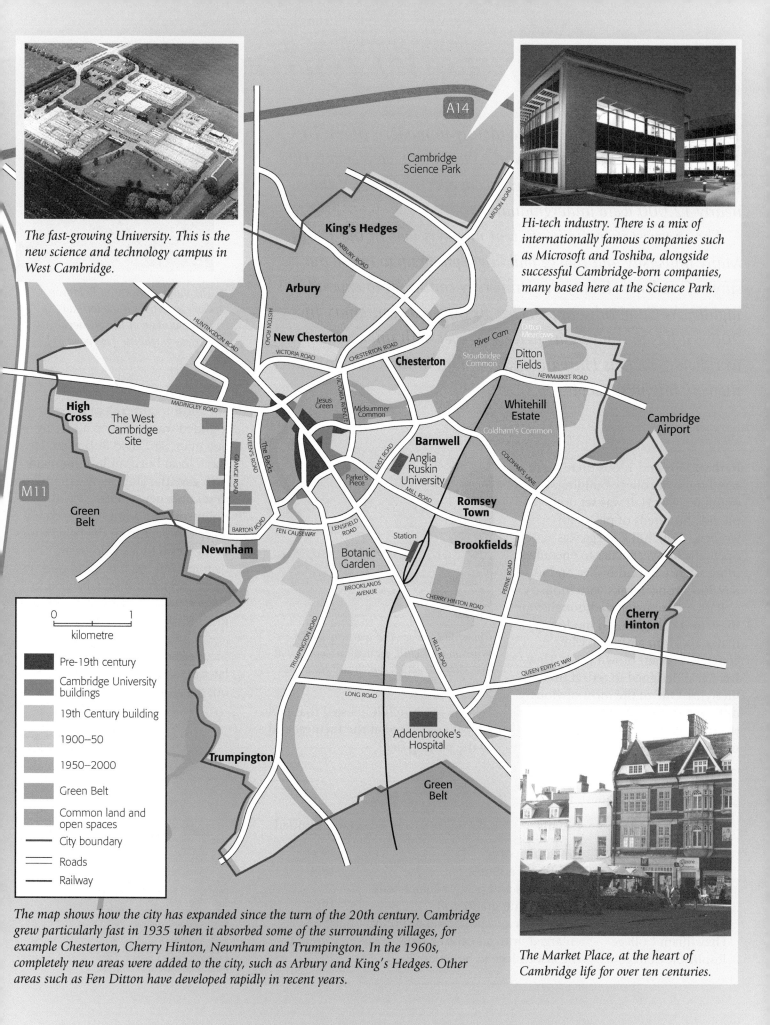

The fast-growing University. This is the new science and technology campus in West Cambridge.

Hi-tech industry. There is a mix of internationally famous companies such as Microsoft and Toshiba, alongside successful Cambridge-born companies, many based here at the Science Park.

A14

Cambridge Science Park

King's Hedges

ARBURY ROAD

Arbury

HISTON ROAD

HUNTINGDON ROAD

New Chesterton

VICTORIA ROAD

CHESTERTON ROAD

River Cam

Ditton Meadows

Chesterton

Stourbridge Common

Ditton Fields

NEWMARKET ROAD

MADINGLEY ROAD

Jesus Green

VICTORIA AVENUE

Midsummer Common

Whitehill Estate

High Cross

The West Cambridge Site

The Backs

QUEEN'S ROAD

GRANGE ROAD

EAST ROAD

Barnwell

Anglia Ruskin University

Coldham's Common

COLDHAM'S LANE

Cambridge Airport

M11

Parker's Piece

MILL ROAD

Romsey Town

Green Belt

BARTON ROAD

FEN CAUSEWAY

LENSFIELD ROAD

Station

Brookfields

PERNE ROAD

Newnham

Botanic Garden

BROOKLANDS AVENUE

CHERRY HINTON ROAD

Cherry Hinton

TRUMPINGTON ROAD

HILLS ROAD

QUEEN EDITH'S WAY

LONG ROAD

Addenbrooke's Hospital

Trumpington

Green Belt

0   1
kilometre

Pre-19th century
Cambridge University buildings
19th Century building
1900–50
1950–2000
Green Belt
Common land and open spaces
City boundary
Roads
Railway

The map shows how the city has expanded since the turn of the 20th century. Cambridge grew particularly fast in 1935 when it absorbed some of the surrounding villages, for example Chesterton, Cherry Hinton, Newnham and Trumpington. In the 1960s, completely new areas were added to the city, such as Arbury and King's Hedges. Other areas such as Fen Ditton have developed rapidly in recent years.

The Market Place, at the heart of Cambridge life for over ten centuries.

The University today

The University has grown tremendously in modern times. In 1938, just before the Second World War, there were over 5,000 students. By the year 2000, there were over 16,000. Of these, nearly 12,000 were undergraduates.

The sharpest increase in student numbers was in the 1960s. Many university and college buildings sprang up to house the surge of students. Today, the University continues to expand rapidly. As Cambridge approaches its 800-year centenary in 2009, it has to compete as fiercely as ever with universities worldwide, such as Harvard and Stanford in the USA, to attract the very brightest people.

The main entrance of Robinson College. This is a modern-day interpretation of the medieval fortress-gatehouse (see page 31).

New colleges and buildings

In the 1950s and 1960s there was a rapid burst of college-building. For example, New Hall was set up to provide hundreds of places for women. Churchill College was opened a few years later to encourage more science in Cambridge and to develop stronger links with industry.

Rather than using traditional stone, these new colleges used modern materials, from gleaming white concrete to plain brown brick. They were also designed to reflect modern lifestyles. One of the most obvious differences was that the chapel, once the focal point of a college, became much less important. In fact, the

Churchill College. The wartime leader, Winston Churchill, planted an oak tree at the college in 1959, which still flourishes today.

Fellows at Churchill insisted that their chapel was placed at the furthest end of the playing field!

Robinson: the most recent college

The most recent college to be founded was entirely paid for by one man, Sir David Robinson. He was a local-born multi-millionaire who gave the University £18 million to set up a new college. David Robinson could not have been more different from the benefactors of medieval times who were bishops, nobles, kings and queens. Robinson left school (the County High School for Boys – now Hills Road Sixth Form College) at the age of 15 to work in his father's bicycle shop in Green Street. He later made a fortune from renting out televisions.

Sir David Robinson gave lots of money to good causes, including a new maternity hospital for the city. It was named after his mother Rosie and opened in 1983.

New colleges in modern times		
College	**Details**	**Date founded**
New Hall	for women only	1954
Churchill College	mainly for scientists	1960
Darwin College	for Fellows and postgraduates only (i.e. no undergraduates)	1964
Wolfson College	for Fellows and postgraduates only	1965
Fitzwilliam College	enlarged from an existing hall	1966
Robinson College	the last college to be set up	1977

Change and tradition

The University has changed tremendously in recent decades. There is now a much greater choice of subjects. Competition for places is fiercer than ever and students have to work hard to earn their degree.

Many ancient traditions have died out. For example, academic gowns were finally abolished in most colleges in the 1960s and 1970s and are now worn only on formal occasions. In 1972, three all-male colleges – Churchill, Clare and King's – finally admitted women. This was considered very bold at the time. Soon all the male colleges saw the benefits of 'going mixed' and followed suit. There are now only three single-sex colleges left (for women): New Hall, Newnham and Lucy Cavendish.

However, many Cambridge traditions have survived, as well as much traditional terminology. A degree course is still called a *tripos*, a new student is called a *fresher* and students enrol in a ceremony called

The University Library is a striking feature on the skyline. It is one of just five 'copyright libraries' in the country. This means that it can claim a free copy of every book published in Britain – from 'A Brief History of Time' to 'Winnie the Pooh'.

matriculation. The week of celebrations following the end-of-year exams is called *May Week*. Strangely, May Week is actually in June! Traditional May Week events include open-air plays, garden parties, the Footlights revue (a student comedy show), madrigals sung from the river and, of course, the famous May Balls.

The University Library

By the early 20th century, the University Library had become too cramped on its existing site in the Old Schools, where it had first opened in 1438. So in 1934, a new library was built, designed by a leading architect of his day, Sir Giles Gilbert Scott. At that time, the new library was considered extremely shocking, particularly with its large, box-like tower. It perhaps comes as no surprise that Scott also designed the Bankside Power Station in London (now the Tate Modern) and the traditional red telephone box!

May Balls are all-night events with dining, dancing, fireworks and champagne, held in some of the most magical settings in the world. Traditionally, after the ball, many revellers punt up the river to Grantchester for breakfast at dawn.

A very traditional scene: students dressed in their gowns for Degree day. In contrast to just a century ago, students are now from a much wider range of backgrounds.

Glittering prizes

Francis Crick's former home in Portugal Place. It is marked by a simple golden helix hanging above the front door.

Cambridge University has a long tradition of attracting some outstanding and creative people. It has fostered great minds which have completely changed our understanding of the world. Pioneers in the University continue to push forward the frontiers of knowledge.

The story of Cambridge's success in science is particularly remarkable. Since it was taught for the first time in the mid-19th century, Cambridge has become a world centre in science. The Nobel Prize, the world's greatest academic accolade, has been won over 60 times by Cambridge scientists between 1901 and 2001.

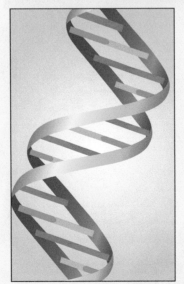

James Watson (left) and Francis Crick

From atomic physics to molecular biology

At the turn of the 20th century, Cambridge led the world in atomic physics. However, after the Second World War, many leading physicists went to work in the USA. America now took the lead. The Cavendish Laboratory instead concentrated its efforts in molecular biology – understanding how living things function. It has had spectacular success in this new field of science. One of the most important advances was made by Francis Crick and James Watson who discovered the structure of DNA.

In 1962, the MRC (Medical Research Council) moved its scientists from the Cavendish to a new laboratory off Hills Road, the Laboratory of Molecular Biology (the LMB). Since then, Nobel prizes have flowed to scientists working there. Prizewinners include Fred Sanger (in 1958 and 1980), Crick and Watson (in 1962), and most recently John Sulston (in 2002).

DNA carries a code for how to build a human. This code was cracked in Cambridge.

Crick and Watson and 'the secret of life'

By the 1950s, scientists knew that genetic information (such as eye colour) was held in DNA, but they didn't know how DNA worked. The race was on among scientists worldwide to solve the mystery. At Cambridge, James Watson, a brash young American and Francis Crick, a talkative British scientist in his mid-thirties, worked together on the problem. They sat in the Eagle pub, just around the corner from the Cavendish in Free School Lane, to discuss their ideas over gooseberry tart and a pint of beer.

In 1953 they finally made their breakthrough. They had worked out the structure of DNA: a molecule shaped like a helix. When cells divided, the DNA could copy itself by simply unzipping the two strands. In this way, there would be a perfect copy of all the genes in the new cell.

Another scientist, Rosalind Franklin (see page 61), a Cambridge graduate, carried out research at King's College London. She did many vital experiments that led Crick and Watson to make their discovery. At the time, Franklin did not receive proper recognition for her brilliant work.

Reading the DNA: a further leap forward

From Crick and Watson's breakthrough, other discoveries in genetics have followed thick and fast. One crucial advance was made by Cambridge scientist Fred Sanger. In 1977, he worked out a method of reading the genetic code on DNA. Scientists could now attempt to read all the genes (the genome) of simple life forms. But it still seemed an impossible task to read the human genome, a sequence of over 3 billion letters long. As late as the 1980s, the technology of the time would have meant 1,500 scientists decoding the human genome for a century.

The Human Genome Project

Luckily, in the late 1980s, scientists discovered speedier methods. They started an ambitious new project – the Human Genome Project. This was biology's equivalent to sending a man to the moon. Much of the work took place in the USA, but the largest single contribution came from the Sanger Institute near Cambridge, which read nearly a third of the genes. In 2003, scientists completed the project to catalogue all the genes in the human body.

Fred Sanger is the only person to receive two Nobel prizes for Chemistry. The Sanger Institute at Hinxton, just outside Cambridge, was named after him. The spiral stairway of the main foyer has been designed to twist like DNA!

Crick wandered into the Eagle pub one February morning in 1953, announcing, 'We have found the secret of life'.

Worm work: John Sulston

Sir John Sulston won the Nobel Prize for medicine in 2002. This was for his research on a lowly, transparent worm less than 1mm long. From his careful and patient research, he saw how the worm's genes controlled the cells dividing and the organs growing. He also observed that sometimes the worm's genes sent instructions to the cells to die. His findings have shed light on human diseases such as cancer (a disease where cells do not die as they should).

From mapping the worm's DNA in the 1980s, Sulston went on to lead the race to sequence the human genome. He was the

Director of the Sanger Institute from 1992 to 2000. He passionately believes that this basic human information should be kept free for everyone's benefit, and not for a few people to get rich.

Looking to the stars

From the microscopic to the telescopic, Cambridge has also played an important part in advances in astronomy. In the last few decades, Cambridge has particularly pushed forward frontiers in cosmology – the study of the origins of the Universe.

In the 1950s, Cambridge was at the forefront of many exciting developments, including radio astronomy. This is the study of very distant stars which cannot be seen with a telescope but can be studied by the faint radio waves they send out. It was pioneered by the physicist and Nobel prizewinner, Martin Ryle, who identified radio galaxies billions of light years away. His discoveries convinced him that the Universe began with an explosive Big Bang.

Excellence all-round

As well as promoting academic success, the University encourages its students to enjoy many other activities, ranging from croquet to choral singing, paragliding to chess. Many undergraduates take such pursuits very seriously and some even go on to win international fame.

Astronomy is one of the oldest subjects taught at the University. When it was studied here in the 13th century, the Ancient Greek belief that the Earth was at the centre of the Universe held sway. Most cosmologists now believe in the idea of the Big Bang – that the Universe began as a colossal fireball over 15 billion years ago.

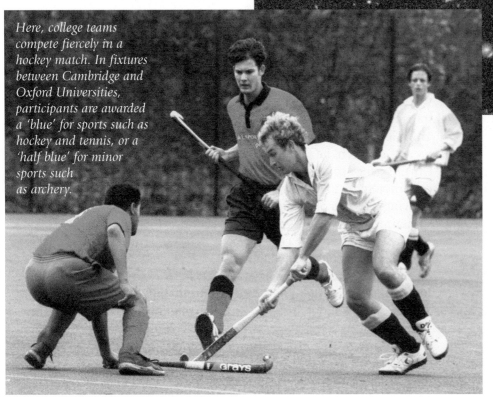

Here, college teams compete fiercely in a hockey match. In fixtures between Cambridge and Oxford Universities, participants are awarded a 'blue' for sports such as hockey and tennis, or a 'half blue' for minor sports such as archery.

The world-famous physicist, Stephen Hawking. He has been Lucasian Professor of Mathematics at Cambridge since 1979, the post once held by Sir Isaac Newton. His popular book 'A Brief History of Time' was a remarkable best-seller.

Cambridge is renowned for its student drama in particular. Best-known of all the students' drama clubs is Footlights.

Footlights

From humble beginnings in 1883, Footlights is now probably the most famous comedy drama club in the world. It reached its heyday in the 1960s, with a stream of highly original writers and performers. One of the most sparkling was a Pembroke student, Peter Cook. In 1961 he co-wrote and performed in the hit comedy, *Beyond the Fringe* with Jonathan Miller, and two Oxford graduates, Dudley Moore and Alan Bennett. The show played to packed houses.

There is a long list of Footlighters who have since become household names. In the 1960s, Eric Chapman, Eric Idle and John Cleese made their names in

Emma Thompson, whose interest in drama flourished whilst at Newnham in the late 1970s. She was the first person in Academy Award history to win Oscars for both acting (in 'Howards End') and screenwriting ('Sense and Sensibility').

Monty Python's Flying Circus. In the 1970s, Bill Oddie, Tim Brooke-Taylor and Graeme Garden found fame through another comedy show, *The Goodies.* In the 1980s there was a further crop of talent with Stephen Fry, Emma Thomson, Tony Slattery and Hugh Laurie.

'Beyond the Fringe' in performance.

John Cleese, who came to study Law in 1960. He is famous for his comedy shows such as Monty Python *and* Fawlty Towers.

The ADC is the oldest university dramatic society in England. Set up in 1885, it performs in this playhouse in Jesus Lane.

Ian McKellan made his name as a Shakespearean actor and later a film star too. Recently he performed in 'The Lord of the Rings' in which he played the Wizard, Gandalf.

As well as Footlights, there are two more well-known drama clubs in Cambridge, the ADC (Amateur Dramatic Club), and Marlowe Dramatic Society. The Marlowe specialises in producing Elizabethan and Jacobean plays and has encouraged many young student actors to make their careers on the stage, including Derek Jacobi, Ian McKellan, and Sir Peter Hall, who is now a very successful director.

The working city

For many centuries, the University has dominated Cambridge. Today, most of the city is linked either directly or indirectly to the University.

Since the 1960s, a new and highly successful area of work connected to the University has been hi-tech science-based industry. This industry is becoming even more important to the local economy than the University. There are now over 35,000 people working in hi-tech companies in and around the city.

The Cambridge University Coat of Arms.

Industry in Cambridge today

There is very little manufacturing in Cambridge. The overwhelming majority of people working in the city (over 90 per cent) work in the service industries.

The largest single industry in the city is education, employing nearly 25 per cent of people. They work in schools, colleges, language schools and the two Universities. These are the University of Cambridge and, since 1992, Anglia Polytechnic University (APU). The University of Cambridge is the largest single employer in the city.

Most people in Cambridge work in service industries. Addenbrooke's Hospital now employs about 6,000 people. This makes it a very important employer in the region. On the hospital site there are an additional 5,000 people working in university medical departments.

The University

The University employs over 7,000 people in academic posts as teachers and researchers, as well as in non-academic posts, ranging from bursars and butlers to technical staff and gardeners. Indirectly, the University has encouraged many other industries too. These include publishing (at Cambridge University Press), setting examinations (at the University of Cambridge Local Examinations Syndicate, or UCLES), teaching English as a second language, tourism and retailing (shops selling to the University and students). The most recent and remarkably successful industry to be added to the list is hi-tech industry.

Tourism brings seasonal work for local people, ranging from punting visitors to selling ice creams.

Cambridge University Press, the oldest publisher in the world, and one of the largest academic presses. This is the Pitt Building, the traditional headquarters of CUP. Near the station is a much larger, modern site where books are published and printed.

The summer invasion

Before the First World War, Cambridge used to grind to a halt during the long university vacations. Shops closed when the colleges closed; the town centre was deserted. Nowadays, as the 16,000 university students depart, the city's numbers

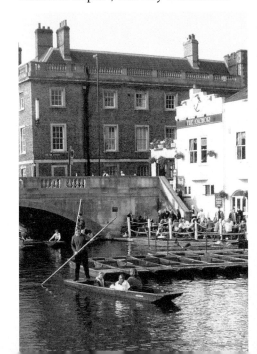

are swelled by tens of thousands of language students, tourists and business people attending conferences. They bring life and prosperity to the city.

Tourism is a major industry for Cambridge. Every year, over three million tourists flock to enjoy the colleges and the Backs. The top attraction is King's College Chapel. In the height of summer, King's Parade is packed with visitors and tour guides. Although the sheer numbers can cause problems, the tourists bring vital income to the city.

Language schools have become big business in Cambridge. Since the 1940s, foreign students have been drawn to the city – as an international place of learning – to study English as a second language. The numbers have grown from a trickle to a flood as English has become the world's international language for business and science.

Language students from all over the world enjoy Cambridge. They help to create a lively and cosmopolitan atmosphere in the city.

The business of science

In the 1960s, the Government urged all universities to make much greater use of their expertise in science. From this sprung the idea of a science complex in Cambridge, where scientists could share their latest research with industry. Trinity College backed the idea enthusiastically and suggested a suitable site: a large, derelict plot of land near Milton (which had last been used in the Second World War to prepare US tanks for the D-Day landings in Europe!). It was here that, in 1970, the Cambridge Science Park was born. The first company to move in was Laser-Scan, started by scientists from the Cavendish Laboratory.

There are now over 1,200 hi-tech companies in the Cambridge area. Most are involved in computing and biotechnology. Over 60 are concentrated in the Science Park. The growth has been so dramatic and fast, especially in the 1980s and 1990s, that it has been dubbed 'The Cambridge Phenomenon'. The computer giant, Microsoft, is one of the latest companies to be attracted to Cambridge.

Silicon Fen

Cambridge has been nicknamed *Silicon Fen*, a small-scale rival to *Silicon Valley*, the world centre for electronics and computing in West California.

Why has Cambridge been so successful? First, there was already a world-class university here with a strong reputation for science. Secondly, the University has been forward-thinking and allowed discoveries made here to be exploited by Fellows and graduates, who have set up their own companies.

Since the 1980s, Cambridge has also had much better communications and this has helped hi-tech companies to flourish. The improvements in road, rail and air links include the M11 motorway to London, the A14 (connecting Cambridge to the West Midlands and east coast ports) and the new terminal at Stansted Airport.

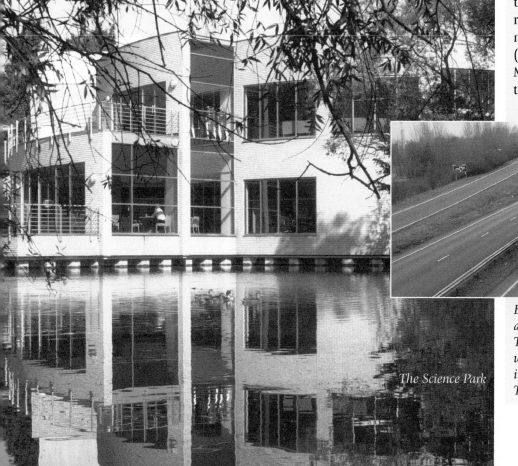

The Science Park

Before the 1960s, Cambridge was a small city at the heart of a rich farming region. Transport links with the rest of the country were poor. Since the late 1960s, hi-tech industry has taken off spectacularly. Transport links have improved dramatically.

Changing places

Cambridge has changed dramatically in the last 100 years. The pace of change has been greater from the mid-20th century onwards than at any time in the town's history. In the 1960s and 1970s in particular, much slum housing was knocked down and many parts of the city were redeveloped.

Some areas of Cambridge, such as the Lion Yard, have changed almost beyond recognition. Others have been enhanced by very gradual change. The Backs, for example, remain a lovely setting for one of the most awe-inspiring buildings in the world, King's College Chapel.

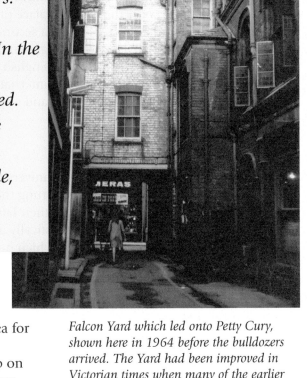

Petty Cury and the Lion Yard

Once a cobbled medieval street selling cooked food and cakes, Petty Cury (or Cooks' Row) has been at the heart of the town's shopping area for many centuries. From medieval times, Petty Cury was also the main thoroughfare from the Barnwell town gate to the Market Place (see map on page 21). Many taverns and coaching inns grew up along its length. These included the Wrestler's Inn, the Red Lion and the Rose and Crown, which Samuel Pepys, the colourful 17th-century diarist, used to frequent. The inns backed onto narrow yards such as Falcon's Yard, Lion Yard and Red Hart Yard, where coaches were unloaded and horses stabled.

In 1972, the old yards and housing, stretching from Petty Cury to Downing Street, were completely demolished in one grand sweep. They made way for a large shopping precinct, a new city library and a multi-storey car park. The redevelopment remains controversial to this day. Many local people are still upset that the area has lost its former charm and character, and maze of historic streets and houses.

Falcon Yard which led onto Petty Cury, shown here in 1964 before the bulldozers arrived. The Yard had been improved in Victorian times when many of the earlier 17th- and 18th-century slums were cleared.

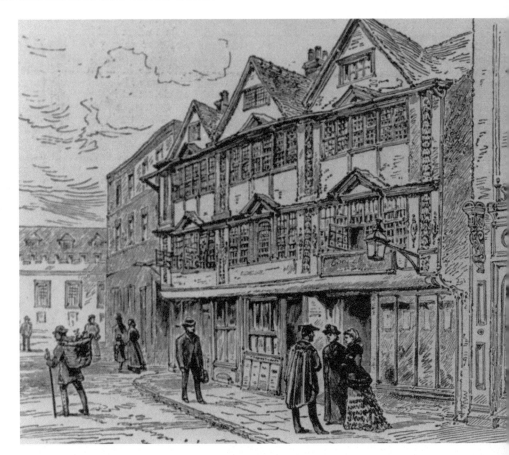

The Wrestler's Inn, Petty Cury, in the late 19th century. Many of the old timber-framed buildings, such as this one with overhanging upper-storeys, were knocked down between the 1880s and 1930s.

Petty Cury seen from Market Square, 1880. The building with the canopy (right) is the old Shire Hall.

Petty Cury over a century later. Nothing in the picture above remains. The Lion Yard extends to the right of Petty Cury. In the foreground is the present-day Guildhall (built in 1936).

In contrast, changes along this stretch of the Backs unfold at a much gentler pace. King's College Chapel (centre) and Clare College (left) are in the background, with the river (hidden from view by the meadowland) flowing from right to left. A punt is just visible to the right!

Index